Routledge Revivals

Economic Development and the Role of Women

First published in 1989, this book provides a macro-micro approach to economic development — taking account of multi-level linkages, both inter and intra, that had been missed by previous analyses. The author argues that these linkages demonstrate that social and economic change may occur from the "bottom up" household/family level and not just from the "top down" economic order level — using women as a vehicle to illustrate this. In the first section, the expansive body of development literature is summarised and critically reviewed — isolating the primary strengths and weaknesses. Case studies of Malaysia, the Chinese Commune and the Israeli Kibbutz demonstrate that a theory which combines the analysis of the organisation of work, kinship and ethnicity can accommodate the experience of women in an integrated manner that traditional development theory has failed to achieve.

Economic Development and the Role of Women

An Interdisciplinary Approach

Ruth Taplin

Routledge
Taylor & Francis Group

First published in 1989
by Avebury

This edition first published in 2017 by Routledge
2 Park Square, Milton Park, Abingdon, Oxon, OX14 4RN
and by Routledge
711 Third Avenue, New York, NY 10017

Routledge is an imprint of the Taylor & Francis Group, an informa business

Publisher's Note
The publisher has gone to great lengths to ensure the quality of this reprint but points out that some imperfections in the original copies may be apparent.

Disclaimer
The publisher has made every effort to trace copyright holders and welcomes correspondence from those they have been unable to contact.

A Library of Congress record exists under LC control number: 89023632

ISBN 13: 978-1-138-23079-8 (hbk)
ISBN 13: 978-1-315-31676-5 (ebk)

Preface for the 2016 Routledge Revivals reissue

This book which was based loosely on my Doctorate from the London School of Economics is fast approaching its 30th anniversary. The issues that are addressed have not diminished in import. There is still a need, perhaps greater than ever, to analyse world development from an interdisciplinary perspective and one that incorporates women and their economic contribution to development in an integrated manner. The family and household continue to remain the underpinning of the world economic order with women making an essential economic contribution to the different levels of household/family, community, nation state and world economic order. This fact which is becoming even stronger by women's contribution to local entrepreneurship through microfinance schemes such as the Grameen Bank and those who are actually now running major corporations/multinationals continues to mean that women are not victims but active players in economic development and always have been. The degree to which women make an economic contribution and are in control of their own destinies does vary according to cultural and historical specificity. Most nation states have different forms of political economy and society which dictates the role that women play to some extent but it does not diminish the fact that women are active participants. This is true for communist dictatorships which still exist today in which women are rarely equal in any way to more capitalist societies where entrepreneurship has allowed more women to become wealth creators and innovators.

The need for a more encompassing conceptual framework in which to analyse the complexities of the economic roles of women at different levels still exists. The combination modes theoretical construct identifies three independent modes which incorporate their own internal dynamics and can be used to define social change in world development in a neutral, culturally and historically specific manner. The three units of analysis of the combination modes approach include the organisation of work, the organisation of kinship and the organisation of ethnicity.

By using the combination modes theory, the nature of social and economic change may be seen in terms of the particular combination of the three modes, including the various levels, found in a specific region of the world at a specific historical time. Social change may be initiated in any of the three modes, at any particular level from either the *top down* for example from the world economic order within the organisation of work or the *bottom up* such as the family within the organisation of kinship. Using this approach, social change may be initiated by one mode at one or more levels, for example social change initiated by change in the organisation of kinship may be manifested at the three levels of the family, household and lineage (clan). Each mode therefore has its own internal dynamic and the change occurs dialectically. This theory continues to have efficacy when determining the role of women in world development which is essential to understanding the vital role women play in the economy and society in terms of carers of the welfare of children and other family members, entrepreneurs, household treasurers, educators and working people in general at all levels of the economy.

The Centre for Japanese and East Asian Studies of which Prof. Taplin is Director won Exporter of the Year in Partnership in Trading/Pathfinder for the UK in the year 2000. She received her doctorate from the London School of Economics and has a GDL in Law. She is the author/editor of 19 books and over 200 articles. She wrote freelance for *The Times* newspaper for 9 years on Japan, Taiwan, Korea and was a consultant to the Federation of Electronics Industry for 9 years

Prof. Taplin was chosen by Routledge in January 2010 as the first author of the month for the whole of Asian Studies and continues to be a featured author. See for a list of her Routledge books https://www.routledge.com/products/9781138935464. Her most recently published books for Routledge are *Intellectual Property Valuation and Innovation: towards global harmonisation* in October 2013 and in February 2016 Managing Cyber Risk in the Financial Sector-lessons from East Asia, Europe and the USA.

She is Editor of *Interdisciplinary Journal of Economics and Business Law* (www.ijebl.co.uk) founded by her and colleagues. Professor Taplin has had a number of visiting affiliations with universities including a Visiting Professor at Osaka City University, Visiting Professor at the Faculty of Management, University of Warsaw, Poland, a Visiting Fellow at the University of Mumbai in January 2007 and in January 2008/April 2009 at the University of Bacheshir in Istanbul. In 2014 she was invited to lecture on IPR in Nepal. She has also worked for a number of law firms specialising in IP around the world on a project by project basis.

Economic Development and the Role of Women

An Interdisciplinary Approach

RUTH TAPLIN
Director of the Centre of Japanese and East Asian Studies, City of London Polytechnic
Research Fellow, University of Exeter

Avebury

Aldershot · Brookfield USA · Hong Kong · Singapore · Sydney

Published by

Avebury

Gower Publishing Company Limited,
Gower House, Croft Road, Aldershot,
Hants, GU11 3HR, England

Gower Publishing Company,
Old Post Road, Brookfield, Vermont 05036
USA

Printed and Bound in Great Britain by
Athenaeum Press Ltd., Newcastle upon Tyne.

ISBN 0 566 07097 9

Contents

Acknowledgements

I would like to thank those persons not already mentioned in the notes for their support and encouragement in completing this work. This book is a culmination of ten years of research, study, paper presentations and article publications and is very loosely related to PhD work completed at the London School of Economics in 1984. Those I wish to thank include Professor John Rex, University of Warwick, Dr. Ian Roxborough, the London School of Economics and Dr.Colin Crouch of Trinity College, Oxford.

An acknowledgement must also be given to Mrs. Jean Baker of the University of Exeter whose careful and efficient assistance in the preparation of the typescript was invaluable to the production of this manuscript.

Finally, if this book only serves to aid the revitalisation of the current stagnation in debate in the important field of development studies it will have fulfilled it's purpose.

1 An overview: top down or bottom up?

The debate concerning world development[1] has been a topical one for several decades. The persistent emphasis on Western biased models of development, men as the predominant social actors and production, provided the reader of the expansive literature with less than an integrative approach. The primary work in the seventies which moved the economic debate in the direction of a holistic argument encompassing men, women and children as social actors who resided in families and households in non-capitalist sectors was Ester Boserup's influential book Women's Role in Economic Development (1970). Boserup's thesis was a radical departure from the assessment of economic indicators based on GNP made by modernisation theory. She argued that GNP does not incorporate non-marketable indicators which include the bulk of women's informal sector, indirect waged, family and other unremunerated "invisible" contributions to the overall condition of a nation's economy. She also emphasised the importance of recognising social historical patterns in different global regions which condition the particular type of wage labour pattern in any given region of the world. The issue of women therefore served to focus on the weak aspects of analysis within the development literature. This is an especially important focus at the present time for the discipline of development because debate has stagnated in general (see Booth 1985) and has not carried Boserup's thesis forward. The inclusion of women, children and gender issues may be utilised to overcome this impasse (Taplin 1989, Sklair 1988, Dixon Mueller 1985). One of the major weaknesses in the bulk of development literature is that in relation to development it has concentrated either on the macro international facets of the economy or the national economy or the community in some cases of the micro-level. In addition, such analyses have consistently argued that social and economic change is directed from the external level of the world economic order. It is such unconnected analyses stressing one level of analysis or another, uniformly attributing change to external, world economic order and subsequently male dominated spheres that is causing an impasse in the discipline. This book suggests that what has been missing from such analyses is a macro-micro approach that takes account of multi-level linkages, both inter and intra. Such multi-level linkages we argue demonstrates that social, economic change may occur from the "bottom up" of the household/family level and not just from the "top down" world economic order level. This form of analysis is encapsulated in the proposed combination modes approach which is both a *methodology* and theory that serves to incorporate the necessary factor of women and children into the development equation as they are mainly concentrated within the bottom sphere of the family and/or household.

Boserup's book initiated a debate that has expanded traditional discussions of the processes of development to include such vital dimensions as gender, ethnicity and the reproduction of the family. The depth of the debate may be seen in the number of different schools of thought that have emerged in the past decade and a half. They include:

1. The historical-materialist school of thought that produced the domestic labour debate which focussed on the theoretical question of whether housework in the broadest sense creates surplus value.
2. The women in development (WID) school of thought which has modernisation leanings is located mainly in the United States and international organisations such as the ILO which views the incorporation of women into the capitalist marketplace as a primary focus for development planning.
3. The world system/dependency school of thought that has very recently recognised the household as a feature of the world capitalist system focusses on the centrality of the Western capitalist (centre) world system showing how the household/women are affected by the world system rather than how the household/women may affect the world system.
4. The cultural anthropological/feminist school of thought which redirected the debate towards the importance of cultural traditions socialisation and psychology in shaping the role of gender and ethnicity within the processes of development.

The expansive body of literature associated with these different schools of thought will be reviewed critically in this book after summarising the diverse constituent parts. A summation of the fifteen year long debates which have attempted to broaden the narrow foci of traditional development literature will seek to clarify gains made in theoretical understanding based on empirical evidence which may be used to move forward the current impasse in the debate. In this particular book women will be used as a vehicle to show the vital necessity of including levels of analyses that focus primarily on gender, ethnicity, the family, household and reproduction for an integrated, holistic understanding of the processes of development and social change.

The critical review of the literature will emphasise both the strengths and weaknesses of the literature. Three primary weaknesses of the current literature will be isolated and addressed in Chapter One. The three major weaknesses that will be addressed in relation to the various schools of thought include:

1. The lack of historical specificity, recognition of cultural diversity and the equal importance of many levels of analysis. These concepts are inter-related in that the history which comprises a unique accummulation of cultural experiences over a prolonged period of time occurs at multi-levels of society. The cultural history, the historically rooted ethnic identity of a nation or region shapes it in a manner that is specific to that nation or region. The household/family level of society is neglected in a number of ways in a good deal of development literature showing a lack of definition and more to the point its importance as a level of analysis. The insistence of many dependency or world system theorists that the societal level of the world economic order is the primary or sole unit of analysis that determines all other forms of historical movement neglects the equal importance of the household/family, ethnic grouping, nation and so forth as a unit of analysis. The capacity for the household level of society to initiate social change from the "bottom up" rather than from the "top down" of the world system level is not recognised by many development theorists. Analyses of women are therefore neglected inherently because female activity is often centred at the household/family level of society rather than at the level of the world economic order.

2. The tendency to perceive particular groups of social actors such as women, peasants, the working classes or specific ethnic groups as passive victims of another group of social actors such as the capitalist classes, men or specific ethnic groups mainly because of a purported rigid, unchanging social structure that perceives one group of social actors as perpetually dominant to another subordinate group of social actors. Mass subordination that is rooted in rigid social structure implies passive victimisation which obscures the reality of the active resisting nature of "victims" lives. Many cultural anthropological/feminist and historical materialist analyses that emphasise the subordination of one group of social actors to another group of social actors explore the victimisation of the subordinated group rather than it's resistance. Both the victimisation of the subordinate group and their resistance to the dominant group demands exploration as they are integrally linked phenomena. Analysis of the resistance of subordinated social groups may provide more vital information than details of victimisation because patterns of resistance illustrate the extent to which the particular social group has been effectively subordinated. The dominant group also demands a more rigourous investigation to determine how it is or if it is victimising the subordinate group. The reaction of the dominant group to the resistance of the subordinate group will demonstrate the intent of the former to victimise and the extent to which the latter group aids its own victimisation and presents itself as the victim. Too often the emphasis of theorists on the victimisation of a social group they deem subordinate amounts to a justification for the political ideology of the theorist.
Women in developing societies are often presented as helpless victims who passively accept their subordinate position to all men in society or an international capitalist class. The evidence shows the futility of portraying all women as universal

victims of men or of an international capitalist class because in many societies they are not subordinate to males and are actually benefitting more for example, from multinational based opportunities than their male counterparts. The woman's role of mother-in-law differs from that of daughter-in-law, for example.

3. A methodological problem exists in a good deal of the development literature because of a lack of neutral categories of analysis free from ethnocentric bias and categorisation. Many theorists tend to analyse other developing societies in terms of their own, projecting ideas about their own society's social organisation in a generalised manner to the society under observation. Phenomena unique to one country are universalised and believed to be common to all nations. In the process of projection these theorists chauvinistically imply that their culture or attitudes are superior to all other social groups. Modernisation theory for example implies strongly in its terms of reference such as modern and traditional which correspond to Western and non-Western societies that modern is good and progressive while traditional culture is less than acceptable, even backwards. Feminists in turn are criticised for universalising and projecting feminist concepts based on Western experience to women in developing societies.

Simply arguing as many neo-Marxist theorists do that social change inevitably emanates and is initiated from the "centre" (i.e. Western capitalist) region of the world is ethnocentric because the West is presumed to be the main influence on the lives of people throughout the world. A neutral set of categories that allows the analyst to explain and understand the constituent parts of the society under observation could be used to circumvent problems of ethnocentric bias.

Towards developing a theory that transcends many of the aforementioned weaknesses a presentation is made of the combination modes theory. This theory identifies three independent modes that incorporate their own dynamics and which may be used to define social change in world development in a neutral, historically specific manner. The three units of analysis of the combination modes approach include the organisation of work and related resources, the organisation of kinship and related resources and the organisation of ethnicity and related resources. It is suggested that none of these organisational modes of society exist in a "pure" form. The specific historical linkages between the organisation of work, kinship and ethnicity in any given society at any particular historical period produces a specific set of circumstances that is manifested at various levels of society and which affects men, women and children equally but differently depending on the level of society at which they are most actively involved with at the time of observation. The three conceptual units of analysis which are manifested at three levels of society include:

1. The organisation of work and related resources (i.e. unearned accumulated wealth and the products of labour power) at the levels of the world economic order, nation state and community.

2. The organisation of kinship and related resources (i.e. children, reproductive activities and human resources) at the levels of the family, household and lineage (clan).

3. The organisation of ethnicity and related resources (i.e. religion, language, art and identity) at the levels of nationality, ethnic groups and tribe.[2]

Using the combination modes theory, the analyst may assess the nature of social change in terms of the particular combination of the three modes (including the various levels) found in a specific world region at a specific period of historical time. Social change may be initiated in any of the three modes at any particular level from either the "top down" (i.e. the world economic order within the organisation of work) or the "bottom up" (i.e. the family within the organisation of kinship). Social change may be initiated in this approach by one or more modes at one or more levels. (i.e. social change initiated by change in organisation of kinship may be manifested at the three levels of the family, household and lineage (clan). Each mode has its own internal dynamic and change occurs dialectically.

The case studies will analyse a number of societies using the combination modes theory as a basis for assessment. Women will be used as a vehicle for this assessment to demonstrate that the combination modes theory can accommodate the experience of women in an integrated manner which traditional development theory has failed to do. The case studies will focus on Malaysia, the Chinese Commune and the Israeli Kibbutz taking into account a variety of historical experiences, political regimes and economics; showing that diversity is so great in the arena of world development that social change may occur from the bottom up or top down in ways unique to the society under observation. Social change is so variable that change may be instigated by women in society, men in society, different ethnic groups or classes or a combination of two or more from all levels of analysis. Before proceeding to the review and criticism of the various approaches, beginning with the modernisation perspective, a diagram is presented below of the "Top-down - Bottom-up" paradigm of social change.

Top-down - Bottom-up Paradigm of Social Change

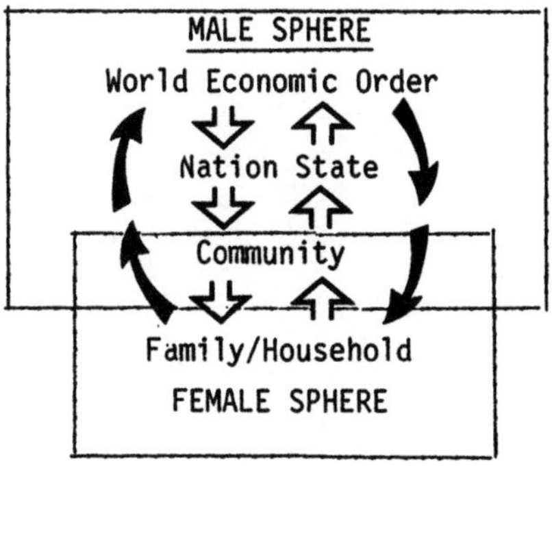

2 Review and critique of the literature and a theoretical proposal

The modernisation approach

Recent theories that have attempted to integrate the role of women into the development literature may be grouped into four broad categories including the modernisation, cultural-dualist, historical-materialist and dependency/sex/gender approaches. Modernisation theory has been one of the more widely known traditional analyses accepted by Western schools of thought which initially inspired criticism by Ester Boserup and subsequent authors.

The modernisation approach supports the idea that women have been in varying degrees subordinate to men; similar to structural-functionalism the formal structures of society that distribute power and authority are seen to determine the position of women in any given society. In what the modernisationists term a pre-modern or simple economy, the emphasis of this research resides with the degree of formal control that women exercise over resource distribution, decision making, services in society, patterns of childbearing and symbolic religious institutions (Freidl 1975). People in simple economies have fewer opportunities for self-advancement than they do in modern societies because of the dearth of occupational specialisation, technology, formal institutions and subsequent lower levels of productivity found in traditional societies. In modern or complex societies the degree of gender equality is measured by the position of women in jural, educational and work structures. Women in pre-modern societies are believed to be subject to patriarchal domination, oppressive childbearing and other family functions. Complex societies are seen to facilitate sexual equality with men, by providing new educational and occupational opportunities that allow access to the formal political-economic structures of society. Greater social mobility coupled with the higher levels of technology of the modern economy make commonplace conveniences such as household appliances and birth control devices that facilitate the participation of women in the formal sectors of society (i.e. Folbre, Ferguson 1981; Sullerot 1971; Freiden 1965). Social change is therefore predicated on upward social mobility into the formal institutions of society coupled by technological advances which move societies forward to modern or complex states of development, determining the position of women. Much of the literature dealing with women and development from a modernisationist perspective shares the belief that the lack of development in Third World nations is caused by the backwardness of traditional society and that the primary problem of Western (modern) development policies is that the benefits of these policies have mainly accrued to men. It is thought that women too require access to the modernised sectors of society. (Eisenstein 1981; Rogers 1981; Loutfi 1980; Zeidenstein and Abdullah 1979; Nelson 1979; Huston 1979; Whyte 1978; Dixon 1978; Epstein 1977; Clignet 1977; Kandiyotti 1977; Lahav 1977; Tinker 1976; Youssef 1974; Hammond and Jablow 1973; Sullerot 1971; Boserup 1970; Inkeles 1969; Kahl 1968; Wilensky 1968; Wood 1966; Weiner 1966; Collver and Langlois 1962).

Western ethnocentrism

The modernisation idea based on evolutionary structural-functionalist thought that all developing societies are in the process of becoming similar to the Western (modern) ideal is challenged for neglecting variation in different world cultures (i.e. Rothstein 1981; Geertz 1973; Goody 1973; Bendix 1970). The tendency of the modernisation approach towards Western ethnocentrism, and a lack of historical specificity is highlighted by its methodological emphasis on teleological progression towards a modern ideal. It is difficult to provide substantive quantitative or qualitative empirical evidence to document changes from simple to complex societies along a continuum while concentrating on the formal institutions of a society which are not uniform throughout all regions of the world. This makes it difficult to substantiate claims for example that male domination has been an integral part of traditional societies.

Many researchers (i.e. Clignet 1977; Kandiyotti 1977; Wilensky 1961) employing this approach place a number of different contemporaneous societies on a continuum scale to demonstrate progression towards complexity. Indicators utilised to assess complexity or higher levels of development tend to rely on generalised statistics such as GNP, mortality rates and educational achievement based on Western economic indices. Assessments of levels of development are predicated on Western models of capitalist industrialisation with socioeconomic indices compiled on the basis of those goods and services that enter a market. The concentration on the formal national market neglects the goods and services that are produced in the household/subsistence sector or other informal sectors often by women or national minorities.

Nash (1976) notes that increased self-sufficiency in agriculture is not viewed as progress by this approach because it can not be quantified in the GNP. Boserup (1970) made the novel argument that the definition of GNP may be extended to include the work of women assessing the overall costs of labour for both men and women within the development process. It is often the case in a number of countries that women, the impoverished and national minorities labour in mainly informal sector work that is remunerated indirectly in the 'invisible' economy of for example homework or is unremunerated in wage form such as subsistence production or family farm work. As GNP is calculated on the basis of what goods and services enter the market of modernised sectors, it would be difficult if not impossible to extend this concept to non-pecuniary earnings. It is arguable whether GNP is a viable indicator of women's economic contribution as it is laden with modernisation concepts and values which define modern, formal market sectors that resemble the West as progressive and all traditional non-waged work and informal sectors as backward. The concept of GNP does not lend itself to multi-level historically specific analysis because it is basically a unit of analysis formulated in terms of production at a world capitalist market or national level restricted to the modern sector. GNP in general provides a restrictive view of economic costs because income distribution and the economic contribution of domestic production at the household level remains masked.

The emphasis on the modern, formal market sectors of developing societies allows modernisation theory to neglect analysis of poor men and women, women who work in the home and in informal sectors and national minorities who engage in informal sector work. In some regions of the world such as sub-Sahara Africa women are mainly concentrated in informal subsistence sectors. European colonial penetration relegated women to informal subsistence sectors, while men were drawn into modern ones in sub-Sahara Africa which blocked structurally the entrance of women into modern sectors. The lack of historical specificity, concentration on formal structures and the evolutionary nature of the modernisation approach prevents this analysis from taking into account historically based structural blockages that do not allow for upward mobility into the formal modern market sectors of certain societies. Rothstein (1982) in her case study of an upwardly mobile peasant community in Mexico noted that she found structural limits to the integration of the peasants into the educational and occupational opportunities afforded by the modern sector in Mexico. While some peasants were unable to enter the modern factory sector, others who did become workers soon found structural limits to their advancement and began to feel alienation from the general consensus found among those in the modern sector.

The importance of the informal sectors - a lack of historical specificity

The concentration on the formal aspects of social institutions does not adequately allow for an assessment of the internal dynamics of the institutions. The household/family level of society is an active facet of the process of social change. Women for example, play important roles in developing societies as the bearers and socialisers of children, as informal mediators of household, village disputes and as subsistence producers who support the base of national social economies through the maintenance and reproduction of family/households. Formalised functions in society are not unequivocally the most significant activities performed by both men and women. In the Middle East and parts of Asia for example, women are involved in the transmission and evaluation of important information through gossip networks, which can have serious implications for the resolution of household or village disputes. Women may use their non-institutional access to power and control, which is commonly channeled through male relations, in a manner that is central to the society they live in (Nelson 1975).

The lack of attention to historically specific detail is directly related to the modernisation approach's lack of recognition of marginalised, informal sectors of society and structural impediments to general advancement of the populace. Progress of the modern sector is defined in terms of the increased educational and occupational opportunities available to all members of society. Developing societies are often compared with earlier stages in advanced industrial Western societies to demonstrate the progress of modern societies. Such comparisons overlook the initial debasement of labour that occurred during the early phases of industrial development (e.g. Engels 1969; Thompson 1963). Etienne and Leacock (1980) show that women who were part of the pre-modern artisan labour force or who fulfilled vital functions in agriculture or cloth-making often lost their valued socioeconomic positions in society when contact with Western capitalism occurred through the mechanism of colonialism. Eisenstadt (1973) argues that because modernisation breaks down ascriptive criteria of status found in traditional societies, all groups in society, including women, exercise greater political power. Nash (1976) notes however that women are often excluded from political parties, especially the higher levels of leadership in both socialist and capitalist developing societies.

Bandarage (1984) notes in a related criticism to Nash (1976) that (what the former terms) the liberal-feminist Women in Development (WID) school of thought believes that the majority of Third World women who live in poverty are aberrations within a social system that is otherwise equitable. Such aberrations the WID school argues may be rectified though legislative reforms, income-generating work or attitudinal changes. Rogers (1980) suggests for example, that the replacement of male development planners by female counterparts could substantially aid women in the Third World. Bandarage (1984) states however, that in real terms such efforts to incorporate women into the formal modern sectors of developing societies has resulted in a limited number of women receiving higher education and salaried employment who would have normally received access to the same opportunities because of their social class. WID efforts according to Bandarage, to for example influence male development planners to replace the males with female planners or to aid women in building their own businesses has not prevented the growth in female poverty, illiteracy and declining numbers of women in the modern sector workforce in many countries.

Neither has modern technological conveniences given women in developing societies greater access to educational/occupational opportunities in the modern sector (Folbre, Ferguson 1981; Sullerot 1971; Freidan 1965). Technology in modern society has instead enabled women to consume ever increasing amounts of gadgetry and styles. Such consumption patterns based on trends and styles maintain wealthier women as professional housewives who do not enter the workplace in modernising sectors of developing societies. Some theorists (i.e. Weinbaum, Bridges 1979; Nash 1976; Mitchell 1971) suggest that the consumerism of modern societies gives an illusion of progress, while encouraging women to become primary consumers who eventually transform themselves into the ultimate consumption object to be bought by men.

Voluntary means less emphasis on victimisation

The modernisation approach based on structural-functionalism does make several unique contributions to our understanding of the process of development and the understanding of women within that process. A primary part of this contribution is the idea of voluntarism, which militates against the presentation of social actors as passive victims, stressing individual choice as some latitude for choosing freely exists to some degree in all societies. Rothstein (1982) noted in her case study of Mexico that social actors will take advantage of opportunities offered by the formal institutions of society within which they live. In Mexico former peasant factory workers operating within the social (Western capitalist) context of occupational mobility through education participated actively in all available opportunities to the extent of making personal sacrifices to have their children advance through education:

> San Cosmeros have not been passive victims of the expansion of industrial capitalism. They are subject to the redivision of the labor force, but they very actively sought to improve the position at least of their children. there are hints that proletarians elsewhere in the Third World are similarly struggling for occupational mobility. If, however, success in the system is as limited as analysis of the new international division of labor suggests, workers as well as behavioral scientists may find the more "refined conceptions of occupational categories" less useful and turn instead to the less refined concept of class (Rothstein 1982:130).

Structural analyses often concentrate so heavily on structure as the determining factor in social change in society that social actors are inevitably viewed as helpless victims whose lives are shaped solely by existing social structure. Modernisation theory focuses our attention on the vital dimension of choice and voluntary behaviour that every social situation allows for to some degree, irrespective of the structural constraints. Although structural-functionalist based modernisation theory facilitates analysis of important individual choices by social actors which militates against the idea that any society is comprised of a mass of choiceless victims, it cannot explain the structural constraints that exist to whatever degree in all social systems. The modernisation approach facilitates analysis of how voluntary choices of business enterprises for example, in relation to management and financial decision making will cause their selection or elimination on the open market on the basis of profit maximisation (Elster 1979). It does not however extend its analysis to the structural constraints that exist at all levels of analysis such as the household level which shapes demand or the world economic order that shapes supply thereby providing a limited perspective of the total social context of analysis that cannot fully explain the position of social actors in a variety of cultures or in historically specific detail.

The cultural-dualist approach

Proponents of the cultural-dualist thesis emphasise factors of cultural-ideology arguing that traditional development literature has failed to note the importance of women's relationship within the nature as opposed to the male sphere of culture and the private/

family sphere as opposed to the male social/public sphere (Weinbaum 1981; Al-Hibri 1981; Phelps 1981; Lindsay 1980; Bourguignon 1980; Chodorow 1979; Weinbaum 1978; Eisenstein 1978; McCormack 1977; Edholm et al 1977; Wadley 1977; Delphy 1977; Oakley 1975; Chodorow 1974; Atkinson 1974; Collier 1974; Rosaldo 1974; Mitchell 1974; Ortner 1972; Firestone 1971; Millet 1969; Levi-Strauss 1971; Freidl 1967; de Beauvoir 1952; Freud 1950).

Adherents of the cultural-dualist approach believe that either women have been excluded from the bulk of the literature concerning development or have been defined narrowly in terms of their biological tendencies (biological reductionism) or in terms of their relation to economic production (economic reductionism). They acknowledge the fact that biological differences exist between the sexes, but it is how these differences are culturally and psychologically translated that accounts for women's unequal position in society universally. This hitherto missing universal cultural ideology which explains the universal subordination of women is termed 'patriarchy'. Patriarchy, the majority who ultilise this term argue (i.e. Weinbaum 1982; Eisenstein 1979; Delphy 1977), is a universal concept that is applicable to the circumstances of women in all societies.

Universal male dominance or patriarchy parallels the creation of society culturally and psychically. Men dominate women universally according to the nature/culture dichotomy because men derived their power initially from exchanging women with non-kin to create inter-familial bonds. Culture began with the exchange of women by men to create bonds between families which caused a fundamental tension between society and the family because the latter was required to relinquish its autonomy. Hartmann (1979) and Ortner (1972) who base their ideas on the writings of Levi-Strauss suggest that the dependency which resulted from inter-familial exchange, created society and ensured heterosexual marriage and the reproduction of the human species. They argue that the sexual division of labour also assures heterosexual marriage because this division of labour constitutes a mechanism that enforces '... a reciprocal state of dependency between the sexes' (Levi-Strauss 1971:347-9). MacKintosh (1981) suggests on the other hand that it is the sexual division of labour itself that causes the subordination of women through gender typing of human beings and the control of women's sexuality within marriage. Meillassoux (1975, 1972) and MacKintosh (1981) both support the idea that women's position in society is shaped by a uniform, universal, transhistorical family/household unit based on male control of women's reproductive capacity. The family is viewed as a fundamental (i.e. Hartmann 1979; Rosaldo 1974; Ortner 1972; de Beauvoir 1952) facet of social organisation in which women reside closer to nature creating dualistic tensions between men and women in the form of an antagonism between nature (family/private) and culture (societal/public). Humans attempt to distinguish themselves from animals through their cultural transcendence because they are not constrained by human reproduction and family susistence. Sexuality (reproduction) and women according to cultural-dualists are associated therefore with nature and are denigrated universally. The dependence of men on both women and nature produces an ambivalent attitude to women. Men's universal celebration and denigration of women is evidenced by Gonzales (1980) and Wadley (1977) in such cultural-ideological dichotomies as the Virgin/Prostitute found in Latin American countries and women as bestower/destroyer in

South Asian Hindu culture. Cultural ideologies are based on the dualistic divisions between nature and culture which explains women's purported inferior position in developing societies.

A variant of the universalist oriented cultural-dualist school of thought (i.e. Weinbaum 1975; Mitchell 1974) views psychological factors as the primary reason for women's universal subordination to men. Mitchell (1974) utilising aspects of Freudian psychology suggests that the universality of the incest taboo facilitated the initial use of women as the exchanged persons at the dawn of human culture, giving rise to patriarchal culture. Patriarchy in relation to this argument refers to fathers rather than all men and cultural laws are believed to be transmitted through the unconscious. Fathers are seen by Millet (1969) to represent universal patriarchal culture because they not only dominate women but younger men establishing male dominant hierarchies based on sex and age.

The argument that fathers embody patriarchal attitudes is based on Freud's (1950) interpretation of the fable of the Oedipal Complex and is used by Weinbaum (1978) in her theories of patriarchy. According to this fable, the father or patriarch of the original primal horde excluded sons from sexual access and control of wives and daughters. The brothers therefore banded together, killed their father and divided the women among themselves, establishing families. At this early period in the development of human culture, the individual patriarchal family replaced the primal horde community. The murderous act of killing the father induced guilt in the brothers, which caused them to atone for their evil deed by demonstrating obedience to a new abstract father; in many cases a God-like deity. Weinbaum argues that these patriarchal values of obedience and submission became incorporated into the social institutions of society, while others because of guilt, obey the patriarchal order with often a religious fervor. Weinbaum supports this contention with examples from Cuba and China, arguing that the father figures of Marx and Lenin and Mao have been elevated to deity-like status.

Chodorow (1974) and Harding (1981) argue that patriarchal culture and attitudes are not only transmitted through the unconscious mind but through gender-specific personality structures that are transmitted within the family. The duties of mothering, Harding (1981) argues are performed only by women who occupy an inferior social position in society which causes the mothering role itself to create men who desire to dominate others. Childrearing practices therefore reproduce personality types that become the socially inferior female mothers who create through mothering dominant males, which is a process that is carried over from one generation to the next.

Erlich (1981) and Phelps (1981) extend the concept of patriarchy to a societal level. They define patriarchy as a whole system of authority structures, in which males exercise universal male authority over females. Power in the form of authority is legitimate, continuous and formalised, while emotional power is not legitimised and is inconsistent within the context of the family. Male power authority, which is the former, originates in and is transmitted through social organisation forms such as the state, which builds unequal access to resources. Limited female power which is exercised in the family can exist within dominant male authority structures, but with less effect.

Leghorn and Parker (1981) suggest an alternative analysis of the power women exercise within universally male dominated social structure. They argue that women experience three levels of power in developing societies which all fall short of significant amounts of power in comparison with universal male power dominance. The three factors that are evaluated within these categories are women's access to crucial resources, the value placed on their reproductive work and the extent to which they are allowed to develop networks. The levels of power that women experience within these categories range from the lowest - minimal - to token and the highest - negotiating power. The developing societies that they describe as pertaining to the three levels of power include; Ethiopia, Peru, Algeria and Japan (minimal), the United States, Cuba and Russia (token) and China, Ewe and Iroquois (negotiating). Despite these different levels of power exercised by women cross-nationally, Leghorn and Parker maintain that even when women exercise negotiating power, they remain subservient to men in all power based relationships and work without compensation for men in the home.

Al-Hibri argues (1981) that men's power drive for authority and control originates with their psychological need for immortality. By controlling resources, biological reproduction and women, men gain access to immortality through generational reproduction of the human species. She suggests that social change occurs dialectically with men attempting perpetually to control women and the latter rebelling against all new forms of male control. The major driving force of history according to Al-Hibri is the male psyche which is the cause of all other oppressions in society. Cultural-dualist theorists such as Al-Hibri (1981), Eisenstein (1978) and Delphy (1977) believe that women's subordination is rooted within the family wherein males may exploit women's capacity for the reproduction of the human species and work.

Weinbaum (1978) and Eisenstein (1978) emphasise the importance of the family by arguing that workers live their private lives in households rather than classes making the family the sphere that socialises both women and men into hierarchical roles based on sex and age. Eisenstein suggests that the universal system of patriarchy has its roots in the culturally transmitted social relation of human reproduction which is based in the family and separate from other social forms. Patriarchy provides its own system of hierarchical ordering and control which is utilised by the prevailing social system.

Cultural-relativism is a distant relation of the cultural-dualist thesis in that it stresses the importance of cultural ideology but is closer to the structural-functionalist argument because theorists of this persuasion (i.e. Bourguignon 1980; Freidl 1975; Collier 1974) analyse the position of women in developing societies in terms of the opportunities and constraints that women experience within the formal institutions of various socio-cultural systems. The majority of women according to this argument adjust to institutional constraints while taking advantage of the opportunities presented by the socio-cultural systems. The Bourguignon volume for example shows that in the contemporary developing society of Saudi Arabia upper class women adjust to their constraints of purdah with a high degree of role satisfaction because they are able to take advantage of the leisured existence, undisturbed by economic worries, offered by their class position. This theory is non universalist in orientation.

Recognising the importance of the family

Cultural-dualist theorists add to the understanding of the position of women in developing societies provided by the structural-functionalist school of thought by creating analyses of interpersonal and informal social structures based in psychology and learned in the family. Cultural relativists add to the structural-functionalist and cultural-dualist perspectives by explaining how women adjust to institutional constraints, especially within the familv.

The emphasis of the cultural-dualist school ot tnought on the family has both increased understanding of the position of women in society and fostered debate generally with regard to the social implications of human reproduction. Prior to the second world war the family, household and personal relations were considered phenomena peripheral to society as a whole. Myrdal and Klein (1957) were among the earliest of the post war women's rights theorists to note that the family/household was a unit of analysis important to both the understanding of the position of women and the operation of society. Mitchell (1971, 1974) broadened the expanding debate surrounding the importance of the family to women and society by redefining the meaning of family within a psychoanalytic and economic context. Subsequent literature which expanded beyond the cultural-dualist school of thought placed the "family" within a conceptual context of ideology. Benston (1969) for example elucidated the importance of the family/household and women's role within the domestic context to the socio-economic structure of the capitalist system. Her argument was based on the evidence that women in Western capitalist societies play an essential role within the family as domestic workers who without remuneration reproduce and maintain the working classes, while serving as a reserve army of potential wage labourers. Morton (1971) underscored Benston's argument by suggesting that the family/household is the primary social institution in capitalist society that produces, reproduces and maintains the working class which supplies capitalism with the essential commodity of labour power. This debate extended itself to the 'Wages for Housework' campaign (i.e. Dalla Costa and James 1975) and analysis of the role of domestic reproduction in the maintenance of the capitalist labour sectors in developing societies (i.e. Deere 1976).

Weaknesses in the concept of patriarchy

The concept of patriarchy which provides the foundation for much of cultural-dualist research is theoretically weak in terms of its generalised universalism and lack of historically specific detail. The universally based psychological force of patriarchy is used to explain all dimensions of society which limits understanding of historically based social transformations from one society to another and cultural diversity. Although the family is emphasised as a unit of analysis, this tendency to generalise extends itself to weaknesses in the definitions of the functions of the family and the meaning of patriarchy in relation to the family. The rigid conceptual division between men and women with the emphasis on women being subordinated to men facilitates the idea of universal female victimisation.

Typologies of social transformation are limited and historically specific detail is lost because all males are viewed as dominant and all women subordinate universally, which excludes societies or aspects of societies that do not exhibit these generalised characteristics. Within the nature/culture dualism all women are considered closer to nature, while men are identified with culture. The diversity of kinship relations in developing societies, evidenced by patrilineal, matrilineal and bilineal descent challenges this perspective. McCormack's (1977) account of the secret religious society of the Sherbo and Mende women of Sierra Leone, is only one empirical example that does not support the nature/culture argument.

Beechey (1979) notes that the foundations of cultural-dualist theory rests on insubstantial evidence as Levi-Strauss does not explain why it is men who exchanged women rather than women who exchanged men. Neither does Freud specify that women were to be exchanged to prevent incest within the kinship unit. Both the Oedipal Fable and Levi-Strauss's theory of the creation of the family unit is difficult to prove. Mitchell's (1974) suggestion that the power of fathers to exchange women accounts for the historical inception of patriarchy is also challenged by Beechey (1979) because fathers do not have this role in matrilineal societies.

The idea of patriarchy because of its universal emphasis lacks clear definition and historically specific detail lending itself to the portrayal of women as passive victims. Patriarchy defined as father-rule or male dominance in general does not apply to all societies as "pure" social formations exist rarely in fact. Rubin (1975) argues that patriarchy as a concept refers to nomadic pastoral societies in which male power is synonymous with fatherhood. Patriarchy defined as a universal, eternal male power drive remains in paradigm form because little uniform analysis exists describing the structural or voluntary properties of male power that produce female subordination and male domination universally. Rape for example, which has been described as a structural feature of a universal, timeless male power drive (Brownmiller 1975) is absent in some societies such as that of the Mbute Pygmies. The Mbute Pygmies as described by the anthropologist Colin Turnbull do not understand the idea of rape.

The methodological problem of conceptualising a uniform universal male power structure is demonstrated by Leghorn and Parker (1981) who acknowledge this theoretical problem by recognising uneven male power because of cultural diversity, while attempting to prove the existence of universal male power dominance. They state:

> Very few of the countries we use to illustrate minimal, token and negotiating power fit solidly into their category. Categories are inherently rigid. So it is important to use them more as a mechanism for freeing our thinking from old concepts and definitions, rather than as something that must be strictly adhered to. (Leghorn and Parker 1981:60).

The discrepancies between their theory and empirical evidence points to a weakness in theory rather than methodology, which sustains its own logic, because their empirical evidence fails to support their theory in a consistent manner. An example of such inconsistency is that although they deem the potential for networking the primary factor affecting female power in society, they cite Algeria as a country exhibiting minimal female power. Algeria, similar to other Middle Eastern Muslim nations, is organised socially in a manner that facilitates strong, segregated female informal networks at all levels of society. Muslim women who are segregated may influence significantly the outcome of important village disputes such as marriages or property rights (i.e. Nelson 1974). As Leghorn and Parker believe that it is through networking women gain an alternative power base, it would seem that informal female network systems in Algeria and other Muslim Arab countries constitute a strong foundation for networking. Leghorn and Parker's theoretical problem in defending concepts of power or patriarchy and locating universal male power structure in society is common to much of cultural-dualist theory. This theoretical weakness extends itself to definitions of reproduction, especially human reproduction within the family. Edholm et al (1977) suggest that three forms of reproduction should be made distinct and separate. They include social reproduction, which is the reproduction of the total conditions of reproduction, reproduction of the labour force and biological reproduction. In my estimation all these aspects of human reproduction are integrally linked and there seems to be little value in separating them for they are all direct functions of the family. An examination of the family in various cultures however can provide vital clues to the role of reproduction and women within societal social structure. Beechey in criticism of this definition of reproduction by Edholm et al states how difficult it is;

> ... to give any rigorous meaning to the various uses of the term reproduction - to sort out... whether biological reproduction should be included within the category of the reproduction of the labour force (or reproduction of labour power), and to understand how to make sense of the control of women's sexuality in terms of the concept of reproduction, I think we have tended to turn to analyses of reproduction in order to avoid a mechanistic version of Marxism which concentrates solely upon the production/labour process, and in order to deal specifically with women's familial activities which Marxism has consistently ignored (Beechey 1979:78).

A clear definition of how human reproduction is organised within the family and its relation to society as a whole is lacking in cultural-dualist analysis. Leavitt points to the vital link between the family and society as a whole which explains the position of women and the role of reproduction in society when she notes;

> The most important clue to women's status anywhere is her degree of participation in economic life and her control over property and the products she produces, both of which factors appear to be related to the kinship systems of a society (Leavitt 1972:396).

Eisenstein (1978) has attempted to define family-based human reproduction through the concept of patriarchy and relate this definition to the organisation of work and distribution of resources in the larger society. In suggesting that the sexual ordering of society which precedes stratified society derives from political and ideological interpretations of functions of human reproduction which men have chosen to exploit politically she begins to construct a concept based in biology but socially interpreted. The resultant social relations of the political and ideological interpretations of women's reproductive functions she defines as patriarchy. She proposes that patriarchy has been culturally transmitted through the family from one historical period to another to maintain sexual hierarchies. Here Eisenstein relates a clearly defined concept of patriarchy to the reproductive functions in the family and defines one of the primary functions of the family as the preservation of sexual hierarchy. Therefore she strengthens the cultural-dualist argument by defining the function of the family in society and relating it in a meaningful way to the concept of patriarchy. However, her argument is weakened when she links patriarchy and the social function of the family to the organisation of work and distribution of resources within a society because she maintains that the former has remained a constant system of sexual hierarchical ordering and male control that has been used historically by different modes of production (the latter).

Eisenstein has weakened a potentially strong argument because she subscribes to the ideal of universal patriarchy based on the subordination of all women by all men that is trans-historical and founded on cultural ideology. To view patriarchy as a cultural ideological relation that provides a system of hierarchical control and ordering that is utilised and transformed by changes in the organisation of work and allocation of resources is to see it as an historical static cultural phenomenon with no internal dynamic. In addition the communal kinship and productive organisation practiced by many matrilineal and bilineal based socieites do not exhibit the patriarchal systems of sexual ordering and male control as explained by Eisenstein. Similar to other cultural-dualist theorists she fails to emphasise the importance of cultural variation. Although the socialisation process in the family may transmit patriarchal attitudes in a variety of forms in different cultures there is evidence to suggest that all socialisation processes in all cultures do not produce patriarchy, especially when defined as the domination of women by men (by implication the victimisation of passive women), in all aspects of society.

This lack of uniformity and universality in the intra-familial socialisation process casts doubt on Harding's suggestion that women today constitute the revolutionary group in history who can transform patriarchal relations by changing personality structures that have been created socially through the universal mothering role. Her argument is based on Chodorow's (1978) analysis of gender linked personality structures formed within the Western family. The suggestions therefore that women may initiate change through gender-resisting practices such as alternative forms of community childbearing is both ill-defined and lacking in sensitivity to cultural variation. Harding does not elaborate on how an autonomous women's movement could provide structural support for alternative infant care that would reshape significantly masculine and feminine personality structures, or to what gender ideal or form personalities would be transformed. Different societies have many different ideas concerning the ideal personality and many developing societies do not accept the women's movement in its present Western (mainly American and Western European) form.

Such lack of definition extends itself to the argument that offers the internal dynamic of social change in the form of a dialectic between new forms of male control and female rebellion. This dialectic offers a possible mechanism of movement but does not explain what would actually constitute a non-patriarchal social form or the specifics of the proposed present dialectic of Al-Hibri's (1981) argument.

Leghorn and Parker's (1981) suggestion regarding the possibility of a transformation to a female form of society in which all women control the allocation of resources and authority functions is also lacking in definition. Female control of social institutions in the place of men they argue, would instill matriarchal cultural-ideology into this new social order and initiate a peaceful egalitarian society. The specifics of this proposed new social order remains unclear as do the special matriarchal characteristics specific to women found in all societies generally. They provide insubstantial evidence to support their idea that all women hold special social characteristics such as cooperation or caring and what these qualities mean or entail in different societies.

The historical-materialist approach

Those theorists using the historical-materialist approach add to both structural-functionalist/modernisation and cultural-dualist models by analysing the material base of society within the context of historical transitions, class structure and the mode of production. (How advances in technology are used depends on the nature of the mode of production). Many theorists of the cultural-dualist persuasion used historical-materialist analysis in their early writings, but became dissatisfied with the lack of emphasis on human reproduction, the family and women inherent in this approach and began their own form of inquiry just reviewed. Other theorists chose not to abandon the foundations of this approach and expanded upon Engels's analysis of the family and women combining these and new insights with the rudiments of historical-materialism, while some have chosen to develop both historical-materialist and family/reproduction centered ideas and integrate analyses of the Third World. All the variations that have basically remained within the broad confines of the historical-materialist approach will be reviewed and criticised below (Ward 1984; Beneria 1982; Hartmann 1981; Joseph 1981; Elson and Pearson 1981; Poewe 1981; Etienne and Leacock 1980; Chipp and Green 1980; Cole 1980; Leon de Leal and Deere 1980; Latin American and Caribbean Women's Collective 1980; Sharma 1980; Buhk 1980; Eisenstein 1979; Beechey 1979; Towner 1979; Papenek 1979; Rapp 1979; Quinn 1977; Chinchilla 1977; Arizpe 1977; Miranda 1977; Stoler 1988; King 1977; Deere 1976; Zaretsky 1976; Leavitt 1975; Saffioti 1975; Rubin 1975; Sacks 1975; Sanday 1974; Rowbotham 1974; Engels 1972; Gough 1961).

Marx and Engels - the roots of historical-materialism

The writings of Marx and Engels provide the theoretical foundation for those utilising the historical-materialist argument to understand the nature of developing societies and how women and the family are an integral but oppressed part of the process of development. The classical theoretical works of Marx and Engels suggest that the process of capitalist development has had an adverse effect on the position of women. The decline in social status that women have experienced in recent history they attribute to the rise of class society, which caused women to lose their position as socially important producers, becoming instead domestic labourers who are bound to the economically isolated nuclear family. Women's inferior position in society is defined in terms of their relegation to the domestic economy and their lack of opportunity to participate in socially productive activity, which consists of the production of goods for society generally. Power relations between men and women and between people in general are located within the context of the mode of production and are based on class structure. To understand the nature of historical development

Marx and Engels focus their attention on those elements in society that control the means of production (i.e. land, tools, factories) and the social relations different sectors of society have to the means of production (i.e. classes). Analysing the changes in control over the means of production is therefore central to understanding the position of women in society.

Engels's (1972) proposes that the division of labour by sex is a separation that has reflected the division of property in society because men owned historically the tools of labour used outside the home. The sexual division of labour has subordinated omen to men because the rise of commodity production and private property has caused privatisation of domestic labour confining female members of the family to the domestic economic sphere. Sanday (1974) notes from this perspective that the sexual division of labour is not inherently oppressive to women for female power in the public domain is related to women's contribution to subsistence, not the fact that labour is divided along gender lines.

Engels's (1972) emphasising the teleological progression towards an advanced mode of production (a socialist one) in which women would enter social production en masse and the nuclear family would no long constitute an economic unit suggests that the pressure to keep inheritable wealth within the family would change with the common ownership of the means of production because of the diminished importance of women as reproducers of male heirs. The household, in which women have become confined would slowly transfer its productive functions to the social sphere. Vestiges of household production, the private sphere of women, would remain until the contradiction of women being impeded from entering social production because of the burden of household duties is resolved by their entrance en masse into socially productive labour. This eventually would leave the household without members to produce domestic services thereby necessitating the communalisation of service production or shared housework. The common ownership of the means of production would provide the basis for a transformation of household service production into social industry, which would remove the final vestige of production from the household, ending the confinement of women to domestic labour (Engels 1972) and changing the organisation of the family and subsequently the nature of society.

An historical understanding of the nature of production but not the family

The strengths of the historical-materialist approach rests with its historically specific understanding of the relation of men and women to the forces of production and the social relations of class structure, the detailed understanding of the mechanisms of capitalist social structure and the concept of dialectical change.

The acceptance of the 'family' as a biological phenomenon that is based on the sexual division of labour which is a natural consequence of sexual differences between men and women presents a major weakness in this approach. Although Engels in particular (1972) made contradictory and incomplete statements regarding the nature of the family in society, his primary analysis of the domestic unit is in terms of a timeless, natural, internally unchanging phenonemon that changes in a manner similar to other natural forms through external impetus. The presentation of the family as a conservative social institution that lacks an internal dynamic requiring an external force to initiate change negates the possibility of the family being an initiator or primary contributor to social change. This tendency to underrate the power of the family level of society as a social force in its own right lends itself to universalistic interpretations of the family and reproduction that are trans-historical and trans-cultural. Such ideas of universalism are linked to Marx's theories of the universal historical transition in stages from one productive system to another such as the universal capitalist system to a universal socialist one.

Criticism of the dearth of rigorous analysis and serious intention given to the family, reproduction and women have been made by a number of theorists within the historical-materialist persuasion. Harris (1980) Bloch and Bloch (1980) and Jordanova (1980) for example, all suggest that nature is used in classical historical materialist writings to justify the subordination of women and the domestic unit in society requires careful scrutiny and demystification.

The idea of Engels that the subordination of women could be ended by the incorporation of females en masse into the wages labour force has been regardedby many as treating the importance of the family and reproductive activities in less than a serious manner. The focus on the family/household as more than a personal phenonemon peripheral to society began with such writers previously mentioned such as Mydral and Klein (1957), Mitchell (1974), Benston (1969) and Dalla Costa and James (1957). The wages for housework campaign facilitated the idea in a tangible form that the domestic unit has its own potential for waged labour because of the importance of its functions and the material contribution of women to society. The notion that the domestic unit is of so little importance to the functioning of society that women need to be drawn into social production for a wage before they may be treated as equals can be viewed as both patronising and a serious underestimation of the importance of the family/household level of society.

Universalism, ethnocentrism, structuralism and populism

The notion that women may gain social equality with men through entering 'social' production and acquiring the conventional male role in society is questioned by Stolcke;

> If women's subordination is attributed to women's exclusion from production, then equality between men and women will depend on women's incorporation into production. But this reasoning is based on the idea that only by making accessible to women the defining attribute of men within the class society, i.e. their non-involvement in procreation and involvement in so-called productive labour, only by converting women into men will equality be achieved... To propose that women have first to become like men in order to become free is almost like suggesting that class exploitation might be ended by making it possible for workers to become capitalists(Stolcke 1981:46).

Stolcke (1981) questions further Engels's explanation of the position of women in society which rests on the purported universal historical overthrow of matrilineal inheritance and subsequent male control of women's reproductive capacities, because men needed to be sure of the mother of their children for inheritance purposes. She argues that such an understanding of the importance of mothers to establishing the legality of child inheritors of the father's property assumes knowledge and an historical valuation of the biological reproductive link. Contrary to Engels's argument she proposes, the social importance of the biological link for class rule by biological inheritors of class position and wealth, emerged mainly with the rise of bourgeois capitalist ideology.

In my opinion, there is veracity in the argument that Engel's speculation regarding universal historically-based male need for control of inheritance and women's reproductive capacity is largely historical projection of the conditions Engels's found in his life experience of nineteenth century Western Europe. In addition, such conjecture is ethnocentric for it imputes the characteristics of nineteenth century Western European social systems upon other countries in the world universally. At the time of Engels's writing other societies held firmly established matrilineal and bilineal societies in which male control of inherited resources was not in evidence or not dominant, which contradicted his argument of the universal overthrow of matrilineal inheritance.

Yet, Stolcke's suggestion that the blood connection for the purposes of inheritance assumed mainly its social importance with the rise of bourgeois ideology is also ethnocentric as other nations throughout history have had pronounced class systems based on patrilineal inheritance. China for example, had a social system based on a feudal-like class structure for centuries that was based firmly on patrilineal inheritance. Traditional Chinese ritual such as ancestor worship, celebration of the birth of a male child, virilocal marriage and lineage family demonstrate the social importance of patrilineal inheritance and a social understanding of the biological link between human reproduction, retention of wealth by certain classes and patrilineal inheritance.

Classical historical-materialist writing has been criticised for extreme structuralism in its analysis of societal social organisation. The often contradictory writings of Marx and Engels have been subject to a number of interpretations but the evidence does point to a structural bias that facilitates the idea of the universal victim.

The tendency of those utilising the historical-materialist approach to view women and the working classes as universal victims has its roots in classical Marxism. The general orientation of the bulk of Marx's work is structural in nature emphasising the process of social change as a consequence of social structure (i.e. the processes of capital accumulation in capitalist societies). Those of the structural-functionalist/modernisation approach that emphasise voluntarism (i.e. social change based on voluntary societal consensus) are the main protagonists of historical-materialist structuralism. However, in some of his writings Marx did suggest that social actors make their own history despite structural constraints. Anglade and Fortin (1985) note that; 'To paraphrase Marx's words, although men's struggles and actions do not take place under circumstances chosen by themselves, but under circumstances directly encountered, given and transmitted from the past; they still make their own history' (Marx 1969 quoted in Anglade and Fortin 1985:24).

Despite this limited acknowledgement that social actors have the ability to make their own history within structural constraints,

Marx did not fully develop the idea of how social actors make their own history while being constrained by social structure. This lack of clear elucidation of how social structure and the freedom of choice of social actors interacts in society has led many historical-materialist researchers to emphasise structural constraints and the plight of the universal worker or female victim. They concentrate mainly on the capitalist class who owns the means of production which limits severely in a structural manner the choices of workers within the capitalist system rather than also emphasising the fact that workers have some degree of choice in selling their labour on a free labour market. This tendency has resulted in many writers viewing the working class as mass passive victims who are dictated to by the capitalist class owned market. In the same manner, feminists, many of Marxist theoretical origin have translated the purported mass victimisation of workers by capitalists to the mass victimisation universally of women by men.

Engels's idea of a point in history when men overthrew the matrilineal order to create a universality based on male control of production, resources and female reproductive capacities lends credence to the view that all women universally are passive victims under the control of men and trapped within the family. Women's reproductive functions and sexuality are viewed as a productive resource to be controlled by men. The working classes are similarly perceived by many of the historical-materialist persuasion as victims who are controlled as a resource by the capitalist classes for their labour power.

Stolcke (1981) likened the absurdity of women becoming similar to men through their entrance into productive labour to the idea of workers becoming capitalists to produce societal equality. In my estimation the central point of this comparison is that in fact Marx and Engels encouraged capitalists to become like workers, which is a rudiment of socialism, while encouraging women to become like men for the sake of equality, which is the epitome of sexism, and a denial of the importance of the family level of society. The power and significance of the family unit to society is quite underrated as is the ability of the family level of society to hinder or initiate social change. In addition, the power that women in many societies exercise through the family in resisting patriarchal orders or foreign colonisation and their domestic contribution to society is dismissed and made trivial.

Finally, the ideas or the interpretations of Marx and Engels that follow the notion of all women becoming like men or all capitalists becoming similar to workers has given rise to populist thought concerning the levelling nature of equality that reduces all individuals to the same state and position universally irrespective of specific ability or merit. Popular socialism and feminism are based on the mass sameness of all members belonging to a popular category such as workers or women. Such populism also rests on the existence of another group of social actors who are presented as the mass universal oppressors that are the root cause of the problems of the social actors of the popular category that believe themselves to be all subject to a similar form of subordination.

The tendencies for historical-materialist researchers to succumb to the theoretical difficulties of universalism, ethnocentrism, structuralism and populism, irrespective of whether such notions do emanate from the classical often contradictory works of Marx and Engels, is clearly manifested in the 'neo-Marxist' literature of dependency, world systems and socialist-feminist theorists.

Dependency/sex and gender approach

A number of neo-Marxist theories that incorporate elements of both the historical-materialist and cultural-dualist approaches to development have emerged in the decades following the Second World War. They seek to explain the nature of development and the position of women in developing societies by relying heavily on interpretations of Marxist or Cultural-Dualist theory or amalgamating the two approaches in various ways.

Dependency theory

Dependency theory and its re-interpreted relation, political economy of the world systems, extend the modes of production analysis of the historical-materialist approach to global levels (i.e. Frank 1975, 1974 (dependency); Wallerstein 1974, 1974; Amin 1975, 1974 (world systems).[3] According to these arguments, historical development is conditioned by the capitalist core of Western nations who own and control the world capitalist market; subordinating the political economies of peripheral developing societies. Dependency theorists believe that the metropolis capitalist nations are slowly and unevenly absorbing the satellite developing societies into the capitalist world market, while world systems writers view the world economic order in terms of a uniform world capitalist system.

The position of women and the household/family level of society has not been addressed until very recently by either strict dependency or world systems theorists. Ward (1984) using regression statistical analysis has shown how the world capitalist system conditions women's fertility patterns in Third World nations. Smith, Wallerstein and Evers (1984) note through case studies of different developing countries how the world capitalist system conditions the economy of households.

Dependency/sex and gender approach

Dependency theorists who incorporate the factors of sex and gender into their analyses, argue that the manner in which the mode of production affects women in developing societies is influenced by the dependent status of the nation in the world system (i.e. Leon de Leal and Deere 1980; Deere 1976; Bradby 1975). They use the concept of modes of production and articulation developed by Rey (1975) and Meillassoux (1972) which suggests that the capitalist mode of production articulates with pre-capitalist modes transforming them in a teleological progression towards a uniform world capitalist system. The articulation or linkage and effect between the capitalist mode of production of core countries and peripheral developing nations may produce a variety of forms of women's productive activities in both urban and rural sectors. Chinchilla (1977) and Leon de Leal and Deere (1980) argue further that it makes little sense to study the changes in women's productive role independent from that of men; in the same manner that they see it as necesary to use the concept of articulation because of the inadequacies of understanding industrial growth in developing societies independent of the international context of capitalist production, investment and control.

Deere (1976) suggests that women in developing societies are drawn into agricultural and urban production because of the requirement of core capitalist nations for the cheapest source of labour to facilitate capitalist accumulation and expansion. More precisely, as the developing world became subordinated to the needs of Western capital accumulation and subsequently a dependant peripheral part of the world capitalist system, women's subsistence production and labour force participation have functioned as a vehicle to drive wages for both men and women below a subsistence wage for individual family workers. Deere (1976) argues that women in developing societies serve a similar function to women in core countries by being available as a reserve pool of labour that enters the capitalist workforce on a temporary basis during harvest seasons or times of war. Unremunerated female subsistence/family work contributes to the survival of the household in periods of unemployment during the capitalist system's cycles of inflation and depression.

Cheap labour

The emphasis of the dependency/sex and gender theorists is on women as cheap labourers who facilitate the process of capital accumulation. The sexual division of labour for example, is viewed as a part of the social structure of society used by capital to benefit the process of capital accumulation (i.e. Buhk 1980; Savane 1980; Stoler 1977; Arizpe 1977; Deere 1976).

Buhk (1980), Leon de Leal (1980) and Deere (1976) suggest that the intra-familial division of labour by sex is a family household survival strategy in developing societies that deals with the socioeconomic conditions imposed on it by the world economic order. Rural and urban poverty is a reflection of the fact that an international capitalist class owns the means of production which forces the dislocation of workers from agriculture at a faster rate than they are being absorbed by industry. Profitability in the capitalist sector according to these theorists depends on low wages and because the capitalist mode of production is often dominant, women are used in such sectors as cheap labour for the purpose of capital accumulation.

Elson and Pearson (1981) view women as exploited by the world capitalist system, especially in terms of low wages, poor conditions and exclusion from the workforce. They argue that women employed by world market factories in developing societies are actually preferred to men because they will work for lower wages and tolerate poorer conditions.

Historical-materialism/sex and gender

Etienne and Leacock (1980) incorporate ideas of sex and gender into the classical historical-materialist approach. They argue that both socioeconomic and sexual hierarchies have developed parallely in history and are inextricably bound for '... it is the relations set up among people as they produce, distribute, exchange and consume the goods upon which they live that are crucial for understanding socioeconomic and sexual hierarchies' (Etienne and Leacock 1980:8).

Sex and gender/historical-materialism

Hartman (1981) and Rubin (1975) who emphasise sex and gender within a broad historical-materialist context suggest that a gender stratification system and mode of production operate dualistically in society with separate dynamics and material bases. The concept of a sex/gender system was created by Rubin and in my estimation is derived from the ideas of Marx and Engels who pointed to the relationship between biological fact and social manifestation. Engels for example noted the relationship between the biologically based and socially manifested sexual division of labour in society. Rubin's sex/gender system approach, which is utilised by Hartmann, views biology as the material base of human reproduction and is defined as a '...set of arrangements by which a society transforms biological sexuality into products of human activity and in which these transformed sexual needs are satisfied' (Rubin 1975:159). Extending Engels's analysis Rubin notes that the resulting socially defined kinship units based on a biological material foundation produce a variety of kinship structures that may be male or female dominant or egalitarian. Rubin (1975) proposes that patriarchy should be restricted in usage to pastoral nomadic societies in which fatherhood is synonymous with male power, while Hartmann equivocates on this issue according to her argument.

The historical-materialist approach as noted has given rise to a broad number of variants to explain the social organisation of developing societies and the position of women which will be criticised separately below.

Etienne and Leacock (1980) suggest that patriarchy or male dominance emerged with changing social conditions in which men established power over women. They categorise changing production relations that condition historically changes in the relations between socioeconomic and sexual hierarchies into four revolutionary models of society, which include egalitarian, ranked or transitional, pre-industrial hierarchical and industrialist capitalist. With respect to the origins of sexual hierarchy they integrate into their work the idea of Engels that rising inequalities between men and women occurred when the sexual division of labour caused men to be responsible for goods or animals that became important forms of wealth.

Colonialism they argue has been the mechanism of historical movement which has transformed social forms in a teleological progression affecting production relations and interpersonal relations between the sexes, often in an adverse manner.

Colonialism has been a central feature of capitalist industrialised societies and the greater the linkage between fully capitalist and pre-capitalist societies, Etienne and Leacock argue, the greater the increase in socioeconomic and sexual inequalities. They suggest that to understand such linkages, and its dual effects on socioeconomic structures and women, several inter-connected variables need to be analysed including; the political and economic requirements of the coloniser, the nature of the capitalist colonialist society and the particular types of strategies used to exploit the colonised and any strategies of accommodation and resistance used by the colonised.

Female dependency theory?

Dependency theory in general including the world systems analysis, even when extended to women, incorporates the historical-materialist tendencies for universalism, ethnocentrism, structuralism, populism, and underrates the importance of the family/household level of society.

The writings edited by Smith, Wallerstein and Evers (1984) which is one of the first acknowledgements of the family/household level of society by traditional dependency/world systems theorists views the function of the family/household as maintaining the structure of the world capitalist system through capital accumulation. The family/household is viewed as a passive economic supporting level of society (similar to the traditional role of women in patriarchal societies), changed only by external influences from the world capitalist system. This approach is ethnocentric as well as structuralist because all change emanates from the highly structured capitalist world economic order which is based in Western (mainly America) nations.

Ward (1984) concentrates, within a weak theoretical framework, on how the world economic order conditions women's fertility and status, again emphasising the external force of capitalist nations on women. In addition, the weaknesses in using statistical analyses are magnified by a dearth of theoretical understanding or definition of the concepts of patriarchy or world economic order or status.

World systems theorists in general as exemplified by the writings of Wallerstein (1974, 1974, 1974) underrate the importance of the state or family/household level of society because they choose the universalist, generalised world capitalist system as the basic unit of analysis. Individual nations states or communities of households are not recognised as totalities in their own right. Poulantzas (1978, 1978) and Cordoso (1979) note for example the importance of the state as a unit of analysis for understanding the nature of world development. Fortin and Anglade (1985) outline the many roles the state plays in the capital accumulation process between capitalist and non-capitalist sectors of society. The state plays an intermediary role between the household and world economic order levels of society through state intervention which in turn affects the position of women. State initiated labour legislation that regulates women's entrance into the labour force and determines their working conditions shapes the structure of the household and the process of capital accumulation on a world scale. (This example will be demonstrated in the case of women workers in Malaysian electronic factories in the subsequent chapter.

Finally, dependency/world systems analysis lends itself to the idea of victimisation by its characterisation of peripheral nations as dependent victims who are totally controlled by a world capitalist system dominated by international capitalists.

The benefits of adding sex and gender and articulation to dependency theory

The dependency/sex gender analysis (i.e. Deere 1976; Buhk 1980) includes the idea of articulation between capitalist and pre-capitalist formations which allows scope for the inclusion of analyses of sex and gender as well as the family/household level of society. The focus on the points of articulation removes emphasis from the all-encompassing level of the world economic order to expose the nature of non-capitalist formations including the household.

The beginnings of an analysis of household subsistence work and the acknowledgement that household levels of society employ survival strategies independent of the world capitalist system allows for an understanding of the family as a changing social phenomenon capable of resistance to external and internal pressures. The emphasis on the importance of women's subsistence labour and unremunerated familial work recognises the essential centrality of women's informal sector work to the maintenance of social economies in developing societies. There are a number of weaknesses in this approach that are related to its historical-materialist roots.

Functionalism, universalism and passivity

As Giddens (1982) has noted about functionalist based theories in general, (i.e. structural-functionalist and historical-materialist), too great an emphasis is placed by theorists such as Deere (1976) and Leon de Leal (1980) on the market functions of the world capitalist system. All interpretations of the sexual division of labour, women's subsistence work, men's wage labour and the function of the household serve a functional purpose of aiding capital accumulation for an efficient world capitalist market.

The emphasis of dependency/sex and gender theory, similar to dependency/world systems theory in general, is on externally based change with all the impetus for social change emanating from the level of the world economic order. The use of the term pre-capitalist shows a tendency towards universalism because of the inherent assumption that all regions are becoming a part of a uniform universal capitalist order. Therefore, although stressing the function of the family within developing societies and the status of women such assessments remain within the context of functionalism and dependent, universally subordinate relations.

This tendency towards functionalism and universalism is rooted in classical historical-materialism. Molyneux (1985) in noting the importance of women and the family to the modern socialist state for the erosion of the old traditional order, reconstruction and stabilisation of the new form of social organisation, points to the writings of Engels. She notes that Engels' basic argument linking the subordination of women to the historical development of private property and class society has been an accepted part of official socialist policy since its inclusion in the 1920 resolutions of the second Comintern Congress. Although Engels' ideas are promoted officially as the means towards the objective of women's emancipation, Molyneux points to the functional uses of these ideals to the economic development goals of socialist state planners, such as adding numbers to the labour force in nations with labour shortages and increasing political support for the state. She addresses further how state function utilises the power of women and the family to gain initially the political support necessary for the overthrow of the old regime. This period of liberalisation in which women's rights are stressed and oppressive features of the family are attacked is eventually replaced in many cases by a call for a return to traditional family norms and women's roles as wife, mother and consumer of household necessities. In some cases the traditional family form is preserved to aid the goals of the state.

In my estimation, the functionalism of the socialist state as suggested by Molyneux differs litte from the functionalism proposed by Deere (1976) in relation to the use of family labour including women by world capitalist multinational concerns. Both Molyneux and Deere stress external forces, the former the socialist state and the latter the world capitalist system, that change women and the family rather than viewing the family and women as initiators of change or powerful forces of resistance. This emphasis on the passivity of women and the family and on functionalism is linked to tendencies found in dependency theory and rooted in classical historical-materialism outlined in previous pages.

Sex and gender and historical-materialism equals historical-materialism

Etienne and Leacock (1980) although incorporating notions of sex and gender into their theory follow the classical historical-materialist approach. They present a rigid, universal evolutionary model of historical transition which masks historically specific detail and inflexibly cannot take into account multi-dimensional social change. Etienne and Leacock (1980) utilise a teleological approach in their theory of evolutionary universalism which has been aptly criticised by Giddens (1982). Colonialism, because of their heavy dependence on historical-materialist theory, is viewed as the main mechanism of historical movement emphasising once more the importance of external world economic order level factors to the processes of social change. However, in using the concept of articulation they recognise that the colonised are active to the extent that they are also shaped by their own forms of accommodation and resistance, not solely by the strategies of the colonisers. Yet, Etienne and Leacock's ultimate emphasis remains with the active coloniser who is the primary initiator of change, shaping the social, economic and political lives of the subordinate, victimised, colonial subjects.

The victim status ascribed by Etienne and Leacock (1980) to colonial subjects in developing societies is not however as great as other writers such as Elson and Pearson (1979) who present women workers in multinational factories in developing societies as "super-exploited" victims of male patriarchal capitalists. Such women workers will tolerate not only the worst conditions, acquiesce to the lowest wage levels but will also be deceived into participating in beauty contests and other sexist personnel management exercises that are self-denigrating (Elson and Pearson 1981).

Brenner (1977) and Warren (1980) to some extent, have challenged undue emphasis on the victimisation of members of Third World nations by arguing that growth has occurred in developing societies despite multinational investments which seek to maximise profits from workers in the developing world. Brenner notes further that historical conditions specific to developing nations serve to shape the nature of the multinational ventures to the same extent that social relations in developing societies are moulded by multinational investment.

Brenner viewed these historical conditions in terms of the productive relations of class; I would add to these historical conditions the organisation of the family and ethnic groupings.

Brenner's vital point which leads to the idea that the historical and cultural experiences of every society are powerful enough to resist the social, economic and cultural imperialism of dominant nations or empires influencing the effectiveness of the coloniser, has not been fully integrated into the writings of many theorists of the historical-materialist and sex gender approach. Barrett (1980) for example, emphasises a historically specific development of capitalism that varies according to class and culture but within the context of pre-existing patriarchal conditions of domestic life that continue under capitalism. As she does not challenge the notion of teleological progression towards a universal capitalism, Barrett's emphasis underrates the importance of resistance by particular developing societies to Western capitalism. She undermines further the recognition of variations in class and culture in viewing all forms of domestic life in capitalist and non-capitalist societies alike as patriarchal. Differing forms of class and culture are inextricably linked to various organisations of the family which challenges the idea that all family forms are universally patriarchal.

Bennholdt-Thomson who has challenged 'male-chauvinist Marxism' (1981:23) for separating social production from subsistence production attempts to reassess the nature of historical development in a manner that facilitates the sex and gender approach's inclusion of important female subsistence work within a historical-materialist context. She suggests that rather than viewing non-capitalist modes of production as modes that retain independent dynamics they should be seen as non-capitalist forms that constitute a subordinated part of the capitalist mode of production. The subordinated non-capitalist forms may be viewed she believes, as a marginal mass of cheap labourers who are an available reserve of labour for capital and who are produced by the internal dynamic of capitalist accumulation. Subsistence work is therefore similar to domestic labour she proposes because it is non-waged work that contributes to the reproduction of the family which provides waged workers to be exploited through their cheap labour for capitalist accumulation of the capitalist system.

This analysis although attempting to extend the idea of the working class to peasants, artisans and women and to integrate subsistence/household work into the concept of social production, in actuality undermines any notion of historical specificity and fails to explain the nature of the family. Her approach falls basically within the dependency/world capitalist system model which views developing societies as subordinated, "super-exploited" parts of a uniform, universal capitalist system. The concept of articulation is not applicable to her analysis because only one internal dynamic remains in the equation and that is the internal dynamic of capitalism. Non-capitalist societies have therefore been stripped of any independent identity, cultural or historical, and have become faceless tools ('the marginal mass') that are victimised by a universal capitalist system. Women become a part of the marginal mass and their specific position in particular societies is overlooked.[4] Brenner's cogent point concerning the ability of societies to resist and shape the nature of their colonisation is lost completely in Bennholdt-Thomson's analysis and partially in Barretts. The desire to integrate sex and gender into the historical-materialist analysis has tended to overwhelm the specific position of women within that approach and not balance integration with specificity.

Sex and gender systems?

Rubin (1970) tends to balance both integration of women and the family into the development debate and factors of historical specificity through her contribution of the idea of sex and gender systems. Rather than attempting to incorporate concepts of sex and gender into concepts of modes of production, she recognises the different and separate functions of the family by defining its own material base, facets of organisation and internal dynamic. Patriarchy, rather than remaining an ill-defined, nebulous concept, Rubin defines as simply one structure of what she terms the sex/gender system. In my estimation, Rubin acknowledges the importance of the family (and women) as a unit of analysis in viewing sex and gender and kinship as a separate mode allowing it to be analysed and linked to the mode of production on an equal basis.

Hartmann has tended to emphasise patriarchy failing to balance integration of sex and gender and historical specificity into her approach. In her earlier writings (1976, 1979) she viewed patriarchy as an established historical system that constituted male control of the labour of women and children within the family. Although in her later writings (1981) Hartmann incorporates Rubin's idea of a sex/gender system acknowledging that it is impossible to ignore the existence of non-patriarchal systems such as matriarchal horticultural societies, she believes that the material base upon which patriarchy rests is in the control of women's labour power by men. This is manifested under patriarchal capitalism by women being excluded from access to productive resources such as a living wage in capitalist societies. She argues that a family wage represents an alliance between all working class men and the capitalist class. This analysis draws on the extremes of populist universalism and victimisation as all men and capitalists conspire to keep women firmly entrapped within the confines of the home.

Humphries (1976, 1979) offers a more realistic appraisal of women and the family in capitalist society by viewing the maintenance of women as non-waged workers as an historical strategy to limit the control of capital over working class family life. The strength of Humphries's work, that is absent in both Hartmann's and many other sex and gender/dependency/historical-materialist literature, is her recognition of the ability of the family level of society to resist external forces related to production.

Ethnocentrism

A point of criticism that concerns all theorists of the historical-materialist persuasion is that of ethnocentrism which may be defined as a tendency to interpret all social phenomena in terms of one's own culture and experience. Understanding of the position of specific ethnic groups in various societies is contingent upon a thorough analysis of the identity of the particular ethnic group. In developing societies for example, how identity and family organisation shapes a particular ethnic group affects its relation to capitalist sectors and whether they will have a direct involvement in waged work.

Dalla Costa and James (1975) were among the first to link the problems of different ethnic groups to those of women by discussing their shared status as marginalised, unwaged labourers. The inclusion of ethnic groupings in their debate tended to be consumed by general interest in domestic labour.

Greater attention has been given recently to the tendencies for ethnocentrism in the broad based historical-materialist approach.

Joseph (1981) criticises writers such as Hartmann (1981) who believe that patriarchy entails the domination of all women by all men. She challenges such all encompassing generalisations by pointing to the contradictions of race within this context in which men in different ethnic groupings do not dominate all if any women in specific societies. Joseph supports her argument with the experience of black men in the United States, who she argues did not hold a superior or dominant position in relation to black women during the period of slavery.

Hartmann (1981), furthering Rubin's (1975) analysis of sex/gender systems, attempts to incorporate into her ideas of patriarchal capitalism a colour/race system in which materially based biologically created colour is transformed into the social category of race. This idea parallels how materially based biologically created sex is transformed into the social category gender in society. Some theorists although regarding sex and gender as biologically based believe that any connections between race and biology made by social analysts such as Hartmann are purely spurious ones.

> The category 'race' is not a biological one but a social construct; it does not parallel the socially constructed category of gender, since this does at least -however grotesquely distorted in many versions of gender - refer to a biological difference between women and men. The social category of 'race' has no comparable biological referent, and the minor pheno-typical distinctions on which racist ideology bases the social category of 'race' are scientific chimaera (Barrett and McIntosh 1985:26).

In my estimation, in their enthusiasm to prove that they are not 'feminist racists', Barrett and McIntosh deny facts based in reality and miss the fundamental points needed to be raised in such arguments regarding ethnicity. It is a fact that may be viewed visually by any independent observer that people of different races, classes and sexes are physically different from one another in various degrees of physical based manifestations. Women tend to be sexually different from men in their physical reproductive functions and features. Racial groups are physically different from one another in terms of colour of skin and/or other visual appearances such as size, height, or body related characteristics. In the same manner, persons of different classes may also create a variety of physical features. Generations of in-marrying aristocrats who do not engage in physical labour and are consistently well-fed may produce a biological tendency towards persons who are tall with small hands, while generations of in-marrying farmers or manual labourers who are ill-fed may produce persons who are short in stature with large hands. People in class related occupations may inherit in several generations a number of physical appearances. Therefore, rather than concentrate the debate regarding race, sex or class on accepting or denying biological fact, it is prudent in my opinion to centre the debate on how these biological differences are socially interpreted, constructed, manifested and established in human societies. To create a socially based theoretical framework for such enquiries is in my estimation the primary task confronting scholars of historical development. As gender begs further analysis instead of biological facts regarding sex, so too ethnicity requires further analytical attention rather than superficial biological facts related to racial physical appearance which like sex is not a pure distinction in many cases with women and men looking like one another or in the multitudinous cases of mixed racial groups.

The need to explore factors of ethnicity in all its dimensions rather than concentrate on racial distinctions often crudely divided between those who are black-skinned and those who are white-skinned has been noted by Anthias and Yuval-Davis (1983). Anthias and Yuval-Davis propose the ideological construct of ethnic division in response to the generalities of black/white distinctions. They note the complexity of ethnicity which is related to factors of historical specificity and how vital details of understanding different ethnic groups may be lost if all ethnic groups in Britain for example, are placed in crude black and white categories. The extreme importance of concentrating on socially created differences in ethnicity rather than factors of biologically created race are pointed out by Miles and Phizacklea (1982, 1980) who show that Irish and Jewish immigrants to Britain despite their similar physical appearance to the English were 'racialised' in the same manner as those peoples who did not have biologically based white skin. Therefore, issues we are dealing with are those of social interpretation and construction, not biological fact as in this case, which is one of many, whereby biological fact is ignored in favour of social interpretation and political expediency. The concept ethnocentrism refers to the criticism of analysing all ethnic groups in terms of ones own ethnic group, which is deemed superior; it does not refer to analysing all ethnic groups in relation to ones skin colour. Colour as Miles and Phizacklea (1982, 1980) have noted is often incidental to those who exploit ethnic differences irrespective of skin colour.

Barrett and McIntosh (1985) believe however, that the black/white distinction is a valid form of analysis and that in relation to Britain the bulk of racism is directed at black persons which they suggest through implication is because of their black skin colour. They agree with Anthias and Yuval-Davis (1983) that to base their socialist-feminist analysis on physical differences in sex or race would be tantamount to being or promoting sexism or racism. Yet, to distance themselves from feminist and anti-racist movements which they believe is the effect of not mobilising around issues of sex and race also has it problems;

> Of course we can point out that slogans such as 'Black is Beautiful!' or 'Sisterhood is Powerful!' rest on a mistaken perception of the categories of race and sex as unitary, thereby denying the specificity of particular historical conjunctures and the complex inter-relations of ethnicity, gender and class. But the danger of this critique is that it is disabling to the large-scale political mobilization for which such slogans are necessary. The politics generated by this critique of essentialism (however correct it may be at an analytical level) are very precise and local. (Barrett and McIntosh 1985:27).

Once more the central issue does not concern biological facts of sex or race nor analytical accuracy but rather social interpretation based on political expediency.

Discussions of ethnocentrism in relation to writers who are assessing the nature of developing societies and the position of women within the theoretical framework of socialist-feminism have focussed recently on a number of problems that originate with historical-materialism.

Amos and Parmar (1984) criticise Molyneux (1981) for stating that some of the changes that imperialism has brought to developing societies and women may be viewed as historically progessive. They object to any suggestion that imperialism, (mainly from the Western nations), has been favourable to women in developing societies in any dimension. Barrett and McIntosh (1985) criticise heavily Amos and Parma for their assessment of Molyneux's work, arguing that the former's critique constitutes a militant form of cultural relativism, impedes comparative work on women, and views dependency theory as the only applicable theory pertaining to developing societies.

These criticisms of Amos and Parmar (1984) by Barrett and McIntosh (1985) seem confused and do not address the substance of the issues raised by the former. Comparative work assumes many different forms and follows various schools of thought. Amos and Parmar therefore, are entitled to disagree with Molyneux's interpretation of the negative and positive points regarding imperialism, in my opinion, without being condemned as extremists or persons who are attempting to block any comparative research on women.

The idea that Amos and Parmar are only inclined towards dependency theory shows a great misunderstanding of the nature of such theory. Dependency theory, although supporting the view that developing societies are victimised by Western nations, also subscribes to the idea, through its historical-materialist roots, that imperialism is a progressive force that undermines traditional values and will lead ultimately to socialism. This tendency to view imperialism as a progressive force in the teleological progression towards socialism and communism is quite strong in all writings rooted in the historical-materialist model.

The work of Molyneux (1985, 1981, 1980) is rooted firmly in an historical-materialist framework which views an historical movement towards socialist/communist societies as progressive. Molyneux's feminist criticisms of modern day socialist nations contain as well ethnocentric tendencies. One of her studies for example, (1980) criticised Cuban government members for viewing Western feminist ideology as an alien form of cultural imperialism. Molyneux (1980) argues that developing societies, socialist ones in particular, which were not favourable to the feminist ideas of sexual liberation in the form of being able to have sexual relationships outside of marriage, homosexual unions and the right for autonomous female organisation were 'puritanical' and against the liberation of women. This is an ethnocentric analysis because she criticises the non-Western work from the confines of the experience of Western capitalist society. The often inordinate emphasis on sexuality that is found in the West or the importance of sexuality to the political understanding and goals of the Western based feminist movement may not be relevant to many developing societies. This point has been raised by Anthias and Yuval-Davis (1983) and Carby (1982 in relation to Western feminist interpretations of the role of the family universally.

Barrett and McIntosh (1982, 1980) suggest that the family is the seat of women's oppression. Anthias and Yuval-Davis (1983) argue oppositionally that in cases of developing societies where families are kept apart by colonial forces, the family does not represent a major site for the oppression of women. Carby (1982) in response to Barrett (1980), argues even more forcefully that the family may be the most significant social institution to culturally and socially resist racism. She notes further that the most flagrant forms of black female sexual degradation emanates from white racism rather than the black family, and that white feminists in the

West assume that their form of marriage and sexual practices are superior to those found in developing societies. Carby argues that Western feminists are largely unfamiliar with the latter. Finally she argues that the black family has been pathologised by nations such as Britain, exposing a patronising and imperialist approach to different ethnic family forms which Western feminists have incorporated into their theory. The great majority of perspectives within historical-materialist approaches (i.e. world systems, dependency theory), including socialist-feminist show an unhealthy, ethnocentric disregard for the family as a site of resistance and social change.

Class structure and dialectical change

There are several fundamental conceptual strengths found in the historical-materialist approach, which are apparent in the broad number of theories derived from this model. These strengths as discussed include historically specific analysis of the relations of men and women to the forces of production in terms of social class, a precise understanding of especially the mechanisms of capitalist social organisation and other modes of production and the concepts of dialectical change and articulation.

An understanding of how capitalist and non-capitalist social organisations in relation to production interact with one another, shaping each others class structure or social form is vital for an understanding of both capitalist and non-capitalist sectors of developing societies. The concept of articulation, which is related to the continuing process of change embodied in the theory of dialectics, facilitates historically specific analysis of social change between two oppositional social forces that are competing for dominance. Articulation shows how competing social actors are linked in a struggle for dominance and resistance and the resulting effects of that temporary linkage. Dialectics on the other hand demonstrates how those who are resistant to an established social order eventually rise to become the new established social order crushing the old. Both concepts are essential for understanding the nature of social change in developing societies. The former facilitates an understanding of external forces that seem to dominate developing societies, while the latter lends itself more to an understanding of internal resistance by social actors in developing nations. Both concepts are useful tools for understanding how women are involved in the processes of social change through accommodation, submission and resistance.

The combination of modes approach

The combination of modes theoretical approach draws on the strengths of the theories already reviewed and criticisied, while attempting to avoid the weaker elements of analysis. The purpose of this approach is to provide a framework for defining social change in world development in a neutral, historically specific manner that encompasses modes of work, kinship and ethnicity. These modes define how gender, ethnicity and class are socially constructed in society providing an integrative approach that shows how women, ethnic groups and classes are socially defined. Each mode has its own internal dynamic which is a dialectic one that moves the modes along in history. The external mechanism of historical movement that influences these modes in developing societies is that of articulation. External change because of articulation may cause internal dialectical change which may in turn cause external adaptive change of articulation. The two forms of change may trigger one another at all levels of analysis, causing domination, resistance, accommodation or submission to occur among different units of analysis within and between modes. Such analysis allows for a flexible assessment of acknowledging that social change may be initiated or hindered from the "top down" of the world order level of analysis or the "bottom up" from the family level of analysis.

Weaknesses

The weaknesses that this combined approach will endeavour to avoid incorporate all those tendencies found lacking in the preceding four basic theoretical models. These tendencies which have been discussed and criticised in relation to each approach include, a lack of historical specificity, the populist tendency to perceive women, particular ethnic groups and classes as passive victims of a universalised "enemy" force, a dearth of analysis regarding the vital importance of the family level of society and women to processes of social change and ethnocentrism.

Strengths

The strengths of the four theoretical models may be combined and re-interpreted to produce a combination modes theory. The strengths of the four models may be recounted briefly according to approach. The structural-functionalist/modernisation approach stresses voluntarism which credits social actors with the ability to choose despite the structural constraints. The idea of voluntarism emphasises the activity of social actors instead of their passive victimisation which provides scope for analyses of resistance, accommodation and decision making in influencing the outcome of historical events of social change.

The cultural-dualist approach emphasises the interpersonal and informal features of society that are based in psychology and learned within the family. The family is viewed as a level of society that has its own important and powerful societal functions rather than being solely an extension of and manipulated by productive forces. Generally, cultural-dualism has brought attention to and increased understanding of human reproduction, family types, household functions and personal relations. An understanding of the importance of the family level of society facilitates analysis of a vital element of the nature of social change. Cultural relativism on the other hand, provides a culturally specific analysis which stresses the importance of ethnicity in understanding how social actors in different cultures adjust to the institutional constraints of their own specific cultures.

The strengths of the classical historical-materialist approach reside with its analyses of the forces of production especially in relation to capitalism as a mode of production and the social relations to the means of production. The concept of dialectical change provides a clear, concise analysis of the mechanisms of social change in society.

Dependency/sex and gender theory although based on historical-materialism has made its own valuable contribution to the analysis of the nature of social change. The neo-classical idea of articulation which is utilised by some dependency theorists provides a basis for describing the linkage and effect between capitalist and non-capitalist modes of production furthering the understanding of the historical specifics of social change. Some dependency theorists have extended and adapted the concept of modes of production by incorporating into their theories new understandings of such phenomena. Sex and gender theory on the other hand, has made a vital contribution to our enquiry by clarifying and focussing on the idea that social intepretation conditions biological fact making issues of sex and race ones of gender and ethnicity.

Combination modes

These strengths coupled with the expansion of the meanings of various concepts will constitute the combination modes theoretical approach. Instead of this approach being dualistic it is comprised of three independent modes that hold their own internal dialectical dynamics at different levels within the modes. Each mode at any level may be changed externally by another mode through the concept of articulation.

The three modes may be summarised as follows:

1. The organisation of work and related resources (i.e. unearned accummulated wealth and the products of labour power) at the levels of the world economic order, nation state and community.
2. The organisation of kinship and related resources (i.e. children, reproductive activities and human resources) at the levels of the family, household and lineage (clan).
3. The organisation of ethnicity and related resources (i.e. religion, language, art and identity) at the levels of nationality, community and tribe.

Each mode has its own internal dynamic which is a dialectic one that moves the modes along in history. Dialectical change occurs at a social ideological level at any or all of the levels of analysis within a given mode. The social ideology is based on the social interpretation of the materially based organisation of modes. The material organisation of the kinship mode gives rise to the social ideology of gender, while the material organisation of the mode of ethnicity gives rise to the social ideology of race and ethnicity. The material organisation of kinship is based in biology (sex) and ethnicity in biology/geography (colour/geographical location) while the material base of the organisation of work is based in the economy and gives rise to the social ideology of class- and wealth-related hierarchy. Dialectical change represents the ever present tension and conflict between men and women, ethnic social actors of different colours, religions, languages and cultures, and class of wealth related hierarchies within the respective modes of kinship, ethnicity and work at all or any one level of analysis. The struggle between the intra-mode social ideologies constitute an established social ideology being challenged by an unestablished one. This conflict often results in the new social ideology overthrowing the old social ideology and replacing it with the new which eventually becomes established in the social institutions of society.

Articulation refers to the external mechanism of change that occurs between modes, linking the predominant social ideologies of each mode causing a change to occur in each linked mode. Linkage between modes through articulation is a temporary phenomenon that causes an effect to occur but unlike dialectical change it does not cause an cverthrow of an established order directly. External change because of articulation may initiate intra-mode change, but intra-mode change occurs through its own internal dynamic of dialectics. Intra-mode change, however, perhaps initiated by extra-mode change may cause one mode to come into conflict with another facilitating the process of articulation between two or three modes. A destabilisation of an established intra-mode social ideology may cause an extra-mode conflict, with the new established order causing other modes to become destabilised through the process of articulation. Complex social ideological linkages between gender, ethnicity and class occur when external articulation links together two or three modes in a temporary union.

The organisation of work

The organisation of work may be defined in terms of how labour is organised and wealth is distributed within a given society. Wealth may be the product of wage-labour, non-wage labour and unearned accumulated wealth through, for example, inheritance. The means by which labour is organised refers to what is utilised to labour on or with to produce goods and wealth. How the products of labour power are distributed depends on how work is organised in a given society according to social ideology which is based on the material resources available to that society. Social ideology conditions the distribution of the related resources of the organisation of work which shapes the social structure within a specific type of social relation.

Examples of different organisations of work which are not exclusive include the primitive or subsistence, slave, simple commodity, feudal, capitalist and socialist modes with their accompanying social ideologies.

The primitive or subsistence mode organises its labour on an individual basis with a collective clan ownership of land. Land constitutes the means of work and the distribution of the products are based on clan, tribal rules. Social ideology is communally orientated.

The feudal form of organisation has many variations cross-nationally but is in essence organised on a class basis consisting of a peasantry and ruler/landlord/lord. The latter owns the means of work which is the land/animals/tools of labour, allowing the former to utilise these resources of wealth production in exchange for either a proportion of the products of the peasant labourers, ground rent, money or whichever form of tribute is expected in a particular society. Social ideology centers on notions of hierarchy, patronage, patron/client relationships or some other form of social obligation of the ruler to his subject.

Labour in the slave organisation of work consists of the slave owner and the slave, with the essential means of work the slave and whatever resources the slave labours on or with which belongs to the slave owner. All goods produced by the slave accrue to the slave owner. Social ideology emphasises the slave as a dispensible but vital commodity that may be bought and sold to create wealth for the slave owner.

The organisation of work in simple commodity production is based on groups of free small producers of equal status who own both the means of work - land, tools and animals - and the products of their labour. Distribution is based on an equal exchange of commodities. Social ideology centres on the importance of kin groups to the survival of the household producing a family oriented self-sufficiency.

The capitalist form of work is organised on the basis of two classes, the bourgeoisie and the proletariat. The bourgeoisie owns the means of work such as factories and equipment, while the proletariat sells his/her labour power on the commodity market. The goods produced by the proletariats are sold back to them on the commodity market at a higher cost than it has taken to produce the goods. Resulting profits accrue to those that own the means of work and the proletariats have little control over the goods that they produce for the market. Social ideology centres on individualism and the survival of those that are able to successfully manipulate the system for individual gain.

The socialist organisation of work remains ill-defined and a moot point concerns whether work and the distribution of resources is organised by the state or by the collectivity of workers. Generally, the organisation of work and the distribution of resources are organised on a collective basis through worker controlled community based collectives or party controlled state apparatus that operate in the interests of workers. Workers in either circumstance own and control the products of their labour and the means of work collectively, while often through the state. Social ideology concentrates on the collectivity and collective gain for the betterment of society as a whole.[5]

These forms of organisation of work operate at all three levels of the mode of work and may exist in conjunction with one another at any of the levels.

The organisation of kinship

The organisation of kinship refers to the organisation and distribution of kinship and descent within a given society. Kinship, which distinguishes non-kin from kin, defines the number of statuses that members of a kinship unit hold and their inter-relationships as well as control over related resources according to a variety of principles and rules. Descent refers to the unit of consanguineally related kin members that is based in the means of kinship which is the material foundation of human biological capacity for reproducing the species.[6] How kinship is organised and reproductive activities distributed in society depends on the social ideology which prescribes who controls (i.e. male, female or both genders) reproductive activities and how they are divided between the two sexes. Reproductive activities require that human resources are used to maintain the biologically created human products (i.e. children) that constitute the material base of kinship. Reproductive activities which draw on human resources, such as love, emotions in general, psychological characteristics, include childrearing, affective relations, socialisation, domestic tasks and family consumption.

Different forms of the organisation of kinship which are not exclusive include matriarchal, egalitarian and patriarchal societies that are rooted in matrilineal, bilineal and patrilineal kinship relations of descent.

Unilineal descent groups, both matrilineal and patrilineal have several basic characteristics in common. These constant features include women holding the primary responsibility for children, maintenance of the descent group through a rule of exogamy, although smaller clan segments may practice endogamy, and the tendency for adult men to hold varying degrees of authority over women and children.

The most fundamental difference between the two forms of organisation centres on gender related lines of descent. In patrilineal kinship units, the lines of descent, inheritance and authority pass through male kin, who are considered the most important members of the kin units. Male kin solidarity and control of male members is therefore essential for the continuation of the descent line. Female members of patrilineal descent groups may exchange their rights in their natal group with their affinal group and not threaten the solidary of patrilineal kin. Daughters are encouraged to exchange their rights, because their brothers are dependent on their sisters' bridewealth for their own marriages. Women as wives and mothers however, are subject to strict control by their husbands and their husbands' groups because their primary function within the kinship unit is to produce male heirs to continue the descent line. Patrilineal based marriage, in which husbands exercise a high degree of authority and women hold low status positions tend to be stable because wives who are separated from their natal group are dependent on their husbands and husbands' families. Women therefore, exercise authority only as mothers, serving to control their sons' wives and compensate for their lack of authority and security through developing strong affective bonds with their male children.

In matrilineal societies, such as those found in Africa south of the Sahara, although lines of authority pass through males, lines of descent, and inheritance pass through the female line. Control within the matrilineal kin group therefore, has to be exercised over both male and female members, because both functions of authority and group placement are essential for the perpetuation of the matrilineal line. Husbands have less control over their wives than men in patrilineal kin groups because if matrilineal descent groups are to be maintained, the ties of women to their descent groups must supercede their relations to their husbands. Male members of matrilineal societies are also required to give first allegiance to their kin groups because they are needed for authority functions. Marital unions are consequently unstable and the status of father/husband varies to a great degree and in some cases the biological contribution of the husband to the creation of his children is socially ignored by matrilineal societies. The reproductive activities of female group members are of great interest to their brothers because sisters often depend on brothers for authority and management, while brothers depend on sisters for heirs and the perpetuation of the kinship units' descent lines. This does not imply however, that each brother is dependent on each sister. All women may be dependent on a single man, an older brother for example, for a period of time. Male authority therefore, does not comprise a uniform, unbroken force but a fluid, changeable form of authority that may be relatively weak. Schneider and Gough (1961:12) note; 'The inter-dependence of male and female members in matrilineal descent groups is thus primarily a phenomenon of descent groups, not of pairs of persons or pairs of statuses'.

A third descent system is that of bilineal or double descent. In this form of kinship grouping, an individual is affiliated with patrilineal kin for some purposes and matrilineal kin for others. These affiliations vary widely with residence bilocal, or separate; inheritance, title, authority passing through either parent; kin groups crossing a number of tribal as well as linguistic boundaries; and childcare the responsibility of either parent. Fixed property may be inherited through the father's descent group, while moveable property may be inherited through the line of the mother. Within a double descent system the range of kinship arrangements are broad and an equal contribution is possible through both male and female descent lines to kinship organisation (Etienne and Leacock 1980; Sharma 1980; Leavitt 1972; Schneider and Gough 1961).

These social forms of the organisation of kinship may operate at all three levels of the mode of kinship and exist in conjunction with one another at any of the levels.

The organisation of ethnicity

The organisation of ethnicity which is the third constituent mode, may be defined in terms of how ethnic factors are socially interpreted, identified and organised within a given society. The mode of ethnicity is materially based in biological colour and geographical location, which is socially translated into ethnic identity through cultural heritage. The means of ethnicity refers to what is used to create ethnic identity through related resources of cultural heritage. The resources of cultural heritage that shape ethnic identity include customs, religion, language and art. How ethnic identity is socially defined through the resources of cultural heritage and how the related resources of cultural heritage are controlled and organised serves to condition in part the social organisation of a society and its social relations.

The social forms of ethnicity constitute all the features of ethnic identity and resources of cultural heritage that a particular ethnic group possesses. The material base of the social forms of the organisation of ethnicity is founded in biological colour or geographical location (i.e. ancestral or adopted homelands) or both. The different social forms (i.e. the number of different ethnic groups that hold specific ethnic identities) are so numerous that it would prove exhaustive to list all or even a goodly number of these forms.

The English for example, base their ethnic identity on their shared cultural heritage of language, religion, art, literature and customs (i.e. traditional ritual) which constitute the means of their ethnic identity. The means of their ethnic identity is materially based on colour. As different ethnic groups of different colours have settled in England with their own ethnic identities, the English mode is no longer a pure one with some non-English ethnic groups assimilating into the cultural heritage of Britain or purposefully maintaining their own ethnic identity. Those of English cultural heritage have also absorbed some of the social form features of other ethnic identities, but the existence of an English ethnic identity based on cultural heritage and its material foundation exists in theory if not completely in practice.

As in the organisation of work and kinship, it is rare to find a pure social form as social forms converge through dialectical change within modes and the process of articulation between modes.

Articulation between modes

A brief example of how different social forms within the three modes may articulate between modes to shape a specific society may be given in relation to the Chinese example, which will be expanded upon at length in subsequent chapters. The emphasis will show the implications for Chinese women in particular in the process of articulation between the three modes.

China during its feudal, patriarchal and Chinese (Han) social forms of the modes of work, kinship and ethnicity respectively, combined through articulation to produce a specific type of society. The three modes combined to produce a societal system whereby strict control by male members of the patrilineal descent group was exercised over the sexuality and reproductive activities of in-marrying wives to ensure continuity of the patrilineal clan, its authority (kinship), property (work) and Chinese cultural heritage of religion, language and customs (ethnicity). Patrilineal clansmen may have lost control over their blood related female members, but gained total control instead over their in-marrying wives who are required to produce heirs to perpetuate patrilineal descent groups to consolidate patrilineal kinship group's property and to carry on traditional Chinese cultural heritage which are all central to the perpetuation of Chinese society.

Control and ownership therefore over the means of work (i.e. property, animals, tools), the means of kinship (i.e. biological reproduction of descendants) and the means of ethnicity (i.e. Chinese cultural heritage such as customs and language) by Chinese patrilineally related clansmen depends on how effectively Chinese women's reproductive capacity is controlled and kept within the kinship unit. Women operating within the organisation of kinship are central for the generation of inheritance, land use and cultural heritage which allows the three modes to combine to produce a distinctively Chinese society at any given period of history.

Internal dialectical change within modes

Brief examples of internal dialectical change within the three modes include class, gender and colonialism/racism which all constitute differing social ideologies.

Within the mode of work and the social feudal form, dialectical conflict between the different peasant classes and landowning classes occurred with each social relation of work (i.e. class) producing its own social ideology.

Within the mode of kinship and the social form of patriarchy, dialectical conflict occurred between the genders causing interfamilial feuds between mothers-in-law and daughters-in-law and marriage resistance movements with the social relation of kinship (i.e. gender) producing its own social ideology. Within the mode of ethnicity and the Chinese social form dialectical conflict occurred nationally between Western non-Chinese who had settled in China (during the colonial period of spheres of influence) and traditionally between Han Chinese, ethnic minorities and the Hakka Chinese from the Northern regions. The social relation of ethnicity (i.e. colonialism and racism) produces its own social ideologies. Below a model is presented to illustrate the Combination Modes approach.

WORK	world economic order	nation state	community
ETHNICITY	nationality	ethnic grouping in host society	tribe
KINSHIP	Lineage	Family	Household

Each mode of the organisation of work, kinship and ethnicity represents a self-contained unit of analysis showing the three levels of analysis. Intra-mode dialectical change may occur across the model in either direction of the levels and according to the prevailing social form(s). Extra-mode change between modes may occur through the process of articulation up and down the model from top to bottom or bottom to top. This means for example that the mode of kinship may initiate change through the process of articulation with the mode of work from the bottom up rather than the top down of the mode of work always initiating change. The organisation of kinship therefore is centered at the local base or bottom of society providing a foundation of personal closely knit human relations in society, while the mode of work operates at the least personalised or top portion of society in which human relations are the most distant and abstracted. The organisation of ethnicity being one step removed from the personal closeness of the family but which may be viewed as a direct extension of kinship relations on a further abstracted level falls in between the distant human relations of the mode of work and the close human relations of the mode of kinship. In my estimation too many traditional theorists in the development field stress the distant human relations of the organisation of work which has become synonymous with the male public world and have not explored fully the organisation of kinship which is often deemed private and female because of the closeness of human relations within that mode of analysis.[7]

Applying the combination modes approach

In the following chapters I shall be applying the combination modes approach to three different regions of the world that hold different social forms. I hope to demonstrate the neutrality of this approach and how it may serve to explain the nature of societies under observation without the biases of ethnocentrism, universalistic generalisation and political populism. The three regional social groups that I intend to assess in the light of this theory are the towns and rural areas of Malaysia, the Israeli Kibbutz which is agrarian, industrial, highly technologised and the rural Chinese Commune. All three of these regional social phenomena have and are experiencing marked social change. The rural and town areas in Malaysia are experiencing social change because of the introduction of high technology semiconductor multinational firms. The Kibbutz is a unique social experiment in its own right created under extraordinary circumstances, while the Chinese Commune of the Maoist historical period was the result of dramatic change caused by tremendous social upheaval in China.

In terms of our model in the case of Malaysia intra-mode conflict has occurred between the world economic order in the form of capitalist multinational companies and the traditional nation state and community. This conflict has caused extra mode articulation between the work and kinship modes of organisation resulting in intra-mode kinship and work mode adjustments.

In the case of the Kibbutz an intra-mode conflict occurred between the nationalities of Eastern Europe and the Jewish ethnic group which caused the three modes to articulate creating a new social form in each mode which produced a new form of society. The extra-mode articulations however were never resolved and the three modes continue to remain in conflict. In the Chinese case the intra-mode conflicts within the modes of work and kinship resulted in the intensification of the traditional extra-mode conflict between the organisation of work and kinship as the nation state was continually in battle with the lineage families for power and control of the nation's resources and loyalties. Intra-mode conflict before the creation of the Communes in the case of the kinship mode saw conflicts between lineages and families, while in the case of the mode of work conflicts arose through the penetration of the Chinese nation state by Western colonialists and imperialists in terms of trade and economic sanctions imposed by the world economic order. These intra-mode conflicts which resulted in a change in the social form of the mode of work and limited change in the mode of kinship have resulted in extra-mode tension between the organisation of kinship and work.

These briefly applied outlines of the combination modes approach will be expanded in the subsequent chapters, showing how social economic change has been initiated mainly from the "top down" of the level of the world economic order in the case of contemporary Malaysia; the "bottom up" at the level of the family/household in the case of the present day Kibbutz system; and from both directions of "top down" and "bottom up" (world economic order, and family/household respectively) in the contemporary Chinese case.

Notes

1. The term development in this book is utilised in a broad manner referring to the processes of historical movement in society including the political, economic and social aspects. When referring to specific facets of development as used in the literature I will do so in specific terminology explaining the particular implications inherent in such usage. See Rothstein (1982) for an explanation of the importance of distinguishing between the generalised terms industrialisation, capitalist industrialisation, economic development and so forth.

2. Lineage and clan have been defined in the same manner and in subsequent pages will be referred to as lineage because both concepts refer to families that descend from a common ancestral line with the eldest patriarch or matriarch the lineage elder, clan head or chieftain. Ancestry through kinship is of primary importance.

3. Tribes, although they contain clan members include as well non-kin who are part of the same ethnic identity. Examples include the twelve tribes of Israel and the thirty-five tribes of Romans. Ethnic affiliation is of prime importance.

3. For a detailed review and critique of both dependency and world systems theory which is beyond the scope of this present argument see Chapter Two of Women and World Development: a critique of the sociology of development by R. Taplin (1984).

4. In her recent work, Bennholdt-Thomson places greater emphasis on cultural value systems and dignity in her explanations of why Mexican women in Juchitan continue to make a great social and economic contribution to the prosperity of the people in this part of South Mexico. (See Bennholdt-Thomson, V. Women's Dignity Is the Wealth of Juchitan (Oaxala, Mexico). Paper presented at the 12th International Congress of Anthropological and Ethnological Sciences, Zagreb, Yugoslavia 24-31 July 1988.

5. This has been adapted generally from S. Amin (1974).

6. This has been adapted generally from Schneider and Gough (1961).

7. Becker is one of few economists who addresses the importance of the family within the context of it's socioeconomic implications in society. He makes a brief reference to the economic importance of the family to traditional (developing) societies, for example noting that the kinship group in this context acts as an insurance company dealing with the welfare of it's members and protecting them against uncertainty (see Gary Becker, A treatise on the family, Cambridge, Mass. 1981).

1 The Malaysian case: an example of capitalist development

In this case study chapter, I shall analyse the nature of historical based social change in Malaysia which has resulted in the current processes of capitalist industrialisation shaping the position of Malayan women in a manner specific to their part of the developing world.

In accordance with the combination modes theory, I will firstly define the social organisation of traditional Malaya according to each mode. Secondly, I shall demonstrate how extra-mode articulation and intra-mode dialectical change between the three internal modal levels has caused modifications in the structure of traditional combination of modes, which has provided the initial impetus and foundation for future social change. Thirdly, the present day social organisation of Malaysia will be detailed showing the progression to the current formulation of combination modes and accompanying social ideology. The experience of women will be used as a focus that threads through the social historical changes that highlight extra and intra modal movement.

The historical patterns of kinship and work in traditional Malaya

Malaya which included Singapore historically is situated in the territory which is currently defined as Southeast Asia. Indigenous Malays are a Polynesian people with their own ethnically distinct art, language and culture. Their ethnic identity is also integrally linked to their traditional particular forms of organisation of kinship and work.

The majority of villagers in Malaya were traditionally bilineal, with children inheriting property from both parents. Women and men retained their family names. Residence after marriage tended to be ambilocal with married couples living virilocally or uxorilocally in the household of the maternal or paternal parents or in a separate household in the village or the towns. An uxorilocal bias in residence was common however, because in traditional practice women inherited and controlled matrilineally the means of work, which were the rice fields that matrilineal kin worked. Daughters were incorporated into their mothers' mutual aid networks in their early years and were part of established work cooperation by the time they were married. Malayan women had been historically active in agriculture as family workers labouring mainly in the rice fields and as hired labourers when matrilineal kin could not deal with the burden of harvest work. This followed the pattern of the majority of farming women in Southeast Asia (Strange 1981; Boserup 1970).

Matri-kin emphasised strongly reciprocal obligations in terms of labour and goods which were carefully calculated because kin were those members of the village that were relied on for assistance when in need. Malay concepts of kinship obligation have been traditionally strong and if members were rude, unhelpful and unwilling to provide the goods requested by fellow kin, they were made to feel shame (McLellan 1985).

Couples therefore, often moved between uxorilocal and virilocal residences according to their socioeconomic needs and those of the bilineal kindred. Husbands and wives tended to adhere to a sexual division of labour though not a rigid one, with women assuming responsibility for child care, domestic tasks and various facets of production while husbands participated in other aspects of productive activity such as ploughing. The egalitarian nature of family relations was reflected in the fact that children of both sexes were equally valued. Children continue to be referred to as wealth (harta) because they are viewed as a joy to parents during their childhood and constitute security in old age (McLellan 1985). Bilineally linked family households comprised the unit that produced the communally oriented matri-kin who laboured in the rice-centered subsistence economy.

The introduction of Islam

The egalitarian based bilineal kinship, work and ethnic organisation of traditional Malayan society was altered to a certain extent by the introduction of Islamic patriarchalism and feudalism. The incursion of Islamic military forces caused an extra-mode articulation between the modes that were uniquely organised according to Islamic and Malayan social organisations during that period. This extra-mode articulation provided impetus for intra-mode changes which altered Malayan society at a number of the levels of the three modes.

Personal names in the post-Islamic conquest period (after 715 A.D.) adopted a patribias with all children acquiring the surname of the father, altering the bilineal nature of the family. Inheritance, in accordance with Islamic patriarchal norms became biased affecting further the organisation of work and kinship at the levels of the community and family with daughters receiving only one half of their brothers' share of the family wealth. Yet, bilineal and subsistence economy tendencies persisted which resulted in females retaining complete ownership rights over any properties and they continued to be entitled to share of the property of deceased husbands.

Husbands emerged as firm heads of the household and initiators of polygamous marriage and divorce; the latter being a commoner feature of traditional Malay marriage than the former. The Muslim conquest also introduced ideas of honour and shame and obedience to the authority of the husband, but such modifications were softened by pre-patriarchal kinship organisation. Women continued to exercise a large degree of economic independence holding the responsible and valued positions of household managers and treasurers. Relations between spouses tended to remain characterised by affection and mutual respect.

In Malayan villages the traditional division of labour continued with men ploughing the fields and women engaging in farming using traditional hand tools for their duties of harvesting, transplanting and food processing. Both male and female children continued to be valued and the work routine of girls remained part of the matri-kin system.

Ethnically, except for the adoption of the Muslim religion and a number of the above mentioned Islamic customs, the Malay culture at the levels of nationality, ethnic group and tribe remained intact at this historical juncture. The extra-mode articulation with Western capitalism and patriarchy that followed the Islamic conquest period hundreds of years later in the nineteenth century had a far greater impact on Malay culture within a historically short period of time.

The impact of western industrialisation on the organisation of kinship, work and ethnicity

The organisation of the modes of kinship, work and ethnicity have been altered by the historically recent introduction of Western capitalism and patriarchy into Malayan society. Changes in technology and the organisation of work began in the nineteenth century, when the demands of the British economy required a stable source of tin and rubber which the resource rich Malay states were able to provide.

The British economy was in crisis at this historical juncture largely because it needed to renew capital accumulation through the expansion of its empire and partly because it was being challenged by rising imperialist powers such as Germany. The tin-rich Malay states and their tropical fertile soil, which proved conducive to the establishment of rubber plantations, were utilised to supply cheap raw materials for British manufacturing industry (Women in Struggle 1978:24). Singapore, which was at this time a part of the Malay states, was used as a commercial centre, and its natural harbour for shipping raw materials to the West (Wong 1980:1). The extra-mode articulation therefore between the British political-economy and that of the Malay states (including Singapore) occurred initially at the level of the world economic order incorporating the latter into the British Empire. The impact of this incorporation was dramatic and had a marked influence at all levels of Malayan internal modes providing an impetus for uneven intra-modal and social ideological change.

The mode of ethnicity altered at the levels of ethnic groups and nationality as Asian Indian and Chinese labourers were brought into Malaya to work in the rubber plantations and tin mines respectively. With the expansion of the raw materials industry came the requirement for a larger workforce which the new ethnic groups met, but they altered the nature of Malay nationality.

The organisation of kinship was also affected in relation to the organisation of work and the sexual division of labour with male family members being initially drawn into wage work followed by female kin members. During the inception of capitalist penetration, men of all ethnic groups became wage labourers, while Malayan women remained as subsistence farmers. Initially, only Chinese and Indian men were brought to Malaya to work in the mines and on the rubber plantations. The brief period of economic expansion that occurred between the two world wars caused an increase in the demand for rubber on the world market. A greater number of rubber plantations workers were needed at this point and Malayan women entered the waged workforce as rubber tappers (Wong 1980; Women in Struggle 1978; Boserup 1970). Malayan women at this time were also drawn into the opium-pressing industry (Women in Struggle 1978) which manufactured opium derived from India that was often used to flood the Chinese market (Moulder 1977). It is quite likely that the wage labour of these women contributed to the family and strengthened their position in the partially patriarchal kinship unit, but there is a dearth of evidence detailing the effects of women's wage labour on the family at this period.

Another contributing factor to Malayan women's increased activity in production may have occurred because of Arab Islamic revivalist ideas that were brought to Malaya during the latter half of the nineteenth century. In Egypt, a liberal phase was occurring which had reformers interpreting the Koran to help resolve problems of an increasingly modernised society. The Koran was also viewed as a symbol of Islamic nations and was used in that capacity to counter the overwhelming influence of Western imperialism. Mohammed Ali of Egypt, to help facilitate his industrialisation plans, used the Koran to justify encouraging Muslim women to participate in work activity and education.

Mohammed Ali laid the foundations for upper-class women to attend higher education and enter the professions. These ideas came to a more full fruition in the 1920's with the liberal experiment in Egypt (Taplin 1987). There is a dearth of evidence regarding this matter, but it would seem likely that the Malayan intellectuals representing the upper-classes facilitated the entrance of upper-class women into higher education and the professions, which influenced the bulk of the population. Therefore, extra-mode articulation with British imperialism at the level of the world economic order combined with subsequent alterations in the traditional and Islamic influenced modes of organisation to produce a form of historical transition particular to Malaya.

An additional extra-mode historical factor that initiated change in the Malayan context was the Second World War. Malaya was deserted by the British and a Malay people's anti-Japanese guerrilla movement emerged which united all ethnic groups, classes and sexes against the invading Japanese. The internal modes combined at the levels of the family, ethnic groupings and community to give rise to a social ideology of unification which was upheld until after the war. Political organisation continued until after the war and the first national women's conference was held in the capital Kuala Lumpur. The extra-mode articulation between the British Empire and the Malay states at the level of the world economic order reasserted itself soon after the Second World War. Britain's requirements for surplus in the form of resource extraction, funds and American machinery, and technology to boost its post-war recovery led British colonialists to fight against Malayan nationalists to retain control of their former colony. The British crushed resistance from both peasants and workers, installing indigenous political allies in power. By 1957, the British-trained administration was in power and the independent Federation of Malaysia came into existence. North Kalimantan was added to the Malaysian peninsula and separate states within the federation were created. The post-colonial state that was instituted during the colonial period implemented laws through a parliamentary democracy, such as laws to prevent the possession of firearms, strikes, worker organisation or the discussion of ethnic matters which served to protect British investment in Malaysia (Women in Struggle 1978:26).

Consequently, Malayan women's increased participation within the workforce must be seen within the context of British imperialism and foreign investment at the level of the world economic order and internal repression under an indigenous political administration tied to British interests at the level of the nation state. Malaysian women have been increasingly incorporated into productive industry in the past twenty years, which has affected women of different ethnic groups at all levels and kinship organisation at some levels of the combination modes. Foreign owned industry in which Malaysian women have become increasingly employed has expanded, reshaping the Malayan political economy. Western directed development from the point of extra-mode articulation has created structural elements that were functional to its needs. In the case of Malaysia, such development included infrastructure, especially in the natural port of Singapore, heavy government regulation of the workforce and the more recent declaration of certain areas where foreign investment occurs as Export Processing Zones (EPZ's) which includes reduced taxes and other incentives.

As Warren (1980) noted, it is possible for a country to industrialise while connected with foreign capital. This may occur I would argue because each independent mode connected to a social entity has its own internal dynamics that are expressed at the different levels of the modes. Therefore, industrialisation may occur at the level of the community or nation state for example, despite the extra-mode articulation at the level of the world economic order. Singapore, for example, which gained independence from the Malaysian Federation of States in 1905, increased its manufacturing sector at the level of the nation state from 12 to 25 per cent of the country's Gross Domestic Product between 1960-1977, (Wong 1980:1) despite its extra-mode articulation at the level of the world economic order, which Wallerstein for example (1979) argues caused total dependence on Western 'core' nations. Yet, as seen by the work of Cardoso (1979), the extra mode linkage at the level of the world economic order may be a powerful influence on the nation state, community, family/households and different ethnic groups. In Malaysia and Singapore dependence on Western technology is increased through the issuing of patents and licenses. Every dollar that is invested in these countries brings five dollars in return to the investor country in the form of profit (Women in Struggle 1978:26).

Women emerge as workers in expanding multinational firms

Malaysia and Singapore are centres of extensive foreign investment, particularly in the area of the new expanding high technology semiconductor industry. The appeal of these nations to multinational firms may be found in their level of infrastructure which was developed during the colonial period, the relatively educated population which speaks English and the educated semi-trained female labour force that may be hired for low wages. The governments of these countries have encouraged foreign investment by offering tariff incentives such as Export Processing Zones, a workforce controlled by government legislation and legal provisions for women workers that facilitate the meeting of requirements by multinational firms, which make women more profitable to hire. These political administrations believe that foreign investment will introduce new technology and provide employment opportunities for the mass of the populace (Wong 1980; Jamilah 1980a). The consequences of encouraging foreign investment are uneven. Although the extra-mode articulation at the level of the world economic order has altered the organisation of work at the level of the nation state and community by contributing new technology, foreign currency and limited employment opportunities, new obstacles to development have been created coupled with new conflicts within the organisation of the family and ethnicity. Increased debt by Malaysia and Singapore has occurred because capital investments are foreign made and owned ensuring that the bulk of profit is returned to the foreign company. New technology also has its limitations in the context of technological transfer to Malaysia and Singapore because of the high cost and lack of its applicability to native industry. Foreign investment has caused problems within both the organisation of ethnicity and the family. For example, at the level of nationality and ethnic groups, conflicts between the Malayan, Indian and Chinese communities have occurred while the employment of Malayan females by multinational firms has caused tensions, at the level of the family and the household and the community, which will be discussed further on in this chapter.

With relation to the semiconductor industry, which comprises part of a global industrial network, the actual technological research and final stages of assemblage are usually carried out in the West in such regions as Santa Clara's 'Silicon Valley' in California. Semiconductor factories in Malaysia, Singapore and the remainder of Southeast Asia bond, chemically dip and test the silicon chip devices[1] (Grossman 1979:9), performing a small segment of the entire operation. Accordingly, the host government learns little about the overall technological process, and research in the parent company progresses so rapidly that by the time the host country discovers a complete technological process it is usually obsolete. On the other hand, technology that is learned may be copied and used to produce indigenously cheaper versions of computer related components that can be manufactured in Western nations.

In terms of employment opportunities electronics factories have provided immediate employment for relatively large numbers of people, especially women, but in general terms levels of unemployment have not decreased significantly, particularly for men. In contrast to the African experience south of the Sahara, where men were required to work in the industrialised urban centres, while women were largely left in rural subsistence sectors, Malaysian men suffer acute unemployment. In Malaysia, unemployed persons are officially defined as men who register with the labour exchange (Grossman 1978:8-14), so it is likely that actual employment rates for men are even higher because many men do not register as they "work" in informal economic sectors.

The pressures of eroding agrarian structures are causing peasants who have been mainly tenant farmers or small landholders, to migrate to the towns and city for work. In the villages, Malayan smallholdings have been declining rapidly since the late sixties because of the expansion of plantation estates, population growth, land concentration by rich landowning peasants and land fragmentation caused by Islamic rules of inheritance (Silcock and Fisk 1963). Although Malaysian peasant and working women have historically contributed to the household income by labouring on family enterprises, engaging in cottage craft industry, working in the textile industry, on rubber plantations and the colonial opium pressing industry, the historically recent electronics industry has markedly expanded their occupational opportunities. Formerly, it was often the fathers and sons of a family who would migrate from the countryside which could no longer support them to the urban centres to search for work. For a decade it has been women, daughters in particular, who have been migrating to urban areas or industrial sites acquiring jobs with semiconductor firms. These female in-migrants find jobs with electronics firms at a more rapid rate than male counterparts. It has been estimated for example that 67.1 per cent of female migrants obtained factory work within two weeks after their arrival in the cities, with 58 per cent, 12.9 per cent and 12.8 per cent hired by electronics, textiles and garment firms respectively (Jamilah 1980a). Rural women therefore are becoming active in wage employment while men- fathers and sons- either work on the family farm or are often unemployed. Women who work in multinational firms make substantial contributions to their families in the villages (Wong 1980:12; Grossman 1979:14).

In Singapore, which was until 1965 a part of Malaysia, economic development has reached a level that makes it a middle income country. Linkages with Western nations at the level of the world economic order has had a more even effect at all levels of the organisation of work, with the greatest expansion in the area of manufacturing providing employment for a large proportion of the population, a higher standard of living and a larger GDP. Singapore, because of its small size, its natural harbour, sophisticated infrastructure, disciplined young workforce and political stability offered by a single dominant party system, has attracted substantial foreign investment.

As economic development has increased in Singapore, especially during the early sixties and seventies, a corresponding rise in the general standard of living has occurred, with the government providing subsidised social services. By the late seventies 64 per cent of the population were living in government subsidised housing, manufacturing accounted for 25 per cent of the GDP in 1977 and in 1978 females accounted for approximately 33 per cent of the total number of employed persons in Singapore (Wong 1980:1,4,6) The figures for female employment are high even in comparison to the employment rate in many industrialised nations, and the occupational structure is segregated by sex. The majority of female industrial workers as in Malaysia are confined to the electronics, textiles, and garment industries. The majority of women are young, single or young married women.

Women in the Malayan context therefore provide a lucid example of how this particular extra-mode articulation at the level of the world economic order since the Islamic conquest period and through to the more marked changes brought about by Western industrialisation altered their position internally and social ideologically in combination with their traditional position in society at all levels of the combination modes. The reasons that have contributed to Malayan women being preferred workers for world market factories such as electronics is a combination of historically based factors initiated by extra-mode articulation at the world economic order level and change through internal dynamics. Malayan women have practiced traditionally a form of agriculture which has fostered an historical pattern of high female participation. Malayan kinship organisation has produced females receptive to male authority especially since the period of Islamic conquest which introduced ideas of honour and shame. They have also been socialised within the household to perform tasks that require manual dexterity which 'trains' them for delicate manufacturing work. The organisation of work which through Western industrialisation has depressed the value of labour of Malaysian workers through the low valuation of indigenous labour because of the displacement of peasants from land for the purposes of plantation estate creation has made Malayan women a source of relatively cheap labour. In addition, the colonial legacy left Malayan women a more highly educated workforce that speaks English. In subsequent pages I will explore how the combination of historical factors which are based on how the different modes of work, kinship and ethnicity combined at different levels when articulation occurred at the level of the world economic order causing women in the Malaysian case to become preferred workers for world market factories. I will also explore current tensions between the women workers, their families and community showing the internal dynamics of present social change.

Women's traditional work roles and the electronics industry

Electronics related work such as semiconductor assembly has increased in the last decade and is drawing peasants, especially women, from the countryside (Asian Employment Programme 1980).[2] America has become the primary base for multinational electronics firms and at the level of the world economic order has been influencing the direction of investment of Malaysia. Through the Asian Development Bank in 1972, the United States provided capital for example to support an 11 million dollar improvement plan for the Malaysian International Airport in Penang. This financial infrastructural support coincided with the growth of the electronics industry at Penang which relies on air freight to ship electronics components (Siegal 1981; Siegal 1979). Advisors from Harvard University's Development and Advisory Service which is funded by the United States Government's Agency for International Development and the Ford Foundation helped to prepare and train native technocrats who authored and implemented the Second Malaysia Plan (1970-75) which promoted export manufacturing. The Second Malaysia Plan called for the creation of 108,000 new manufacturing jobs and a campaign to attract electronics investment from a worldwide market. The World Bank in 1974 initiated the idea of Export Processing Zones for Southeast Asia which eventually spread to Malaysia (Siegal 1981; Siegal 1979). In 1970, the Malaysian government provided exceptions in the labour laws that protected women from night shift work to meet conditions acceptable for Western electronics plants (Grossman 1979:8).

As noted previously, Malayan women were economically active throughtout history. They were active as household managers, family treasurers and domestic labourers in the home, producing household implements such as baskets and mats. While men ploughed or hoed the fields, women were equally active utilising traditional farming tools and techniques to harvest, transplant and process food. Malay husbands, however, were not adverse to cooking or cleaning if circumstances caused them to participate in domestic duties. The mutal aid networks that mothers developed among female family members and neighbours were essential to the survival of the household. Daughters were integrated at an early age into their mother's network as noted earlier, and married couples often lived uxorilocally in order that daughters could remain within their mother's highly organised female mutual aid networks (Taplin 1983; Strange 1982). Malayan women were traditionally independent economically, often controlling family expenses. Women were entitled to a share of their husband's property upon the death of the latter and exercised total ownership rights over property accumulated before or after marriage (Firth 1966; Djamour 1959).

The majority of rural women continue to engage in traditional farming techniques using hand tools for their duties of harvesting, transplanting and processing food, coupled with plantation waged work. Men rather than women are being introduced to the heavy machinery of the modern farming sector. Pressures on small landholders and increasing landlessness has caused a decline in women's agricultural contribution. Handicraft production based on traditional basket and mat making skills is one economic activity that women are engaging in to supplement the family income. The handicraft industry is either part of an organised government project that pays a wage or is an informal activity performed in the spare time of women at home and given on a consignment basis to shopkeepers for sale. Government sponsored handicraft concerns have not encouraged mechanised weaving because they consider hand weaving a part of the Malaysian heritage. Handicraft production is also conditioned by the world market through tourist demand (Taplin 1984b, 1983; Strange 1981).

Multinationals in the past 15 years have become a significant sector of employment for rural women who commute or migrate to urban areas. Malayan females constitute 55.5 per cent, 56.8 per cent and 89.5 per cent respectively of the electronics, textile and garment industry workforce in Malaysia. The electronics industry in particular is experiencing an impressive rate of growth. In 1970, for example, 41 electronics companies employed 3,200 workers and by 1976 this number had increased to 138 with 47,000 workers employed (Jamilah 1980a:47). With the expansion of the electronics industry, the scope for Malayan women to enter general electronics sector employment is increasing and at a faster rate than that for men. (See Table 1).[3]

Women are 'trained' for electronics work in the family

Malayan women who work in multinational electronics plants are considered to be apprentices up to six months, but usually require only one to two weeks time to learn skills needed to perform their jobs satisfactorily (Heyzer 1982:192; Grossman 1980:10). The ease with which these women learn their occupational skills may be attributed to the early training of females in household based manual dexterous skills taught traditionally within the family. This socialisation process teaches girls to be manually dexterous, patient and to concentrate, which are all required skills for the delicate procedure of silicon chip assembly and testing. The weaving of Pandanus palm leaves into baskets for example is a traditional domestic skill passed from generation to generation. Palm leaf weaving requires manual dexterity and speed as this task has been practiced traditionally by village women in their spare time. The colouring of baskets or mats with dye demands, care, patience and skill (Strange 1981). The skills needed for Pandanus weaving are readily transferred to assembly work in multinational firms. Careful, skilled techniques needed to dye baskets may be transferred to equally careful chemical dipping procedures for testing silicon chips. The quick, efficient weaving of baskets and mats is not very far removed from the delicate bonding of chips procedure, for which production workers are required to slice two to four inch diameter wafers into as many as 500 separate chips. Each chip is then bonded with up to 50 minute strands of gold wire. This work must be accomplished with the utmost skill and speed as individual quotas for binding may exceed 800 chips per day (Taplin 1984a, 1984b; Elson and Pearson 1981; Grossman 1979; Siegel and Grossman 1978). The electronics industry saves training time and maximises profit by utilising skills taught to women within the context of family socialisation. Had Malaysian men been trained traditionally in domestic skills rather than Malaysian women, it is probable that they too would be employed by world market factories such as electronics firms.

World market factory environments often imitate the kinship organisation and expectations of Malaysian families, with male supervisors presenting themselves as father-like authority figures, which is related to the role that rural Malay fathers play within the family (Grossman 1979:5). Marriage is stressed in electronics factories which reflects to an extent the Malaysian family attitude to marriage. Women are believed to be expendable workers, because their employers assume they will marry eventually and that their husbands will support them. It is possible that the managers of the world market factories in Malaysia impute Western ideas of the ideal patriarchal nuclear family to their female employees, as the latter are seen not to be permanently reliant on a wage, in contrast to the male head of the household in Western nations. Electronics companies tend to recruit their workforce from a stratum of young, single daughters who may be used for wage labour before they perform the socially necessary function of child reproduction. The emphasis on marriage and reproduction found in rural Malaysian families is not challenged by the personnel techniques of electronics factories but reinforced through managerial practices which includes fashion and beauty contests. Male supervisors present themselves as father-like authority figures, while the recreational contests and classes serve both as 'fatherly indulgence' (Grossman 1979) and reinforcement of the idea that marriage is the ultimate goal for women. Women in rural Malaysian families are taught to compete for the most desirable males through their beauty and domestic skills. Managerial practices reflect such family emphasis through beauty contests, cosmetic application, sewing and cooking classes and romantic poetry in company newsletters (Lau 1981). The competition among women for marriageable males acquires a new form and aids electronics firms in times of expansion and contraction keeping the labour force through high turnover, flexible and inexpensive (Frobel, Heinrichs and Kreye 1980; Ong 1983), while reinforcing traditional kinship organisation at the levels of the family and the household.

However, it is dubious to argue that the supposed docility or subservience of Malayan women results from an indigenous patriarchal order or gender subordination which is compared to the self-repressed resentment of the colonised people for colonisers (as Elson and Pearson argue 1981:95). Malay family organisation as noted is organised patriarchally to a limited extent, but is based on historical rooted bilineal egalitarian kinship structure. Girls are taught to behave in a respectful, cooperative manner because Malayan families emphasise traditionally mutual cooperation, which is linked to their upbringing as future members of female mutual aid networks from which the livelihood of the household depended historically. Expressions of anger or the personal self-indulgence of temper tantrums are not conducive to the harmonious cooperation of mutual aid work teams. To organise successfully such networks, individual feelings of anger and dissatisfaction must be suppressed. In addition, ideas of honour and shame (related in particular to sexuality) which were introduced into Malaya by Muslim invaders accentuate modest behaviour on the part of Malayan women. Anger and dissatisfaction therefore are culturally expressed through the religiously related medium of spirit possession. Spirit possession which many rural Malayan women experience on a temporary basis is a socially safe manner in which to express feelings or frustrations through screaming, seeing visions or writhing on the floor. These social, safety valve spirit possessions have been transformed into outbreaks of mass hysteria on the factory floor of multinational firms such as electronics (Ong 1983:434-35). Attacks of spirit possession begin in many cases with female workers seeing the spirit of their female ancestors or mothers in their electronic microscopes which causes them to become hysterical, perhaps causing writhing on the floor which then spreads throughout the factory section (Grossman 1979). The respectful, cooperative behaviour of the majority of Malayan women may be misinterpreted as docility and submissiveness, but I believe it is more credibly explained by historical inter-connections between the modes of the organisation of work in the form of matrilineal mutual aid cooperation networks; the family in terms of bilineal kinship which allows uxorilocal residence by the married couple and the restoration of maternally based mutual aid networks; and ethnicity in the particular cultural form unique to Malayans which give rise to the cultural expression of anger, especially among females in terms of religiously related spirit possession.

Malayan women as cheap labour?

Malayan women are often seen as preferred workers by multinational firms because they will work for low wages as will their other Southeast Asian counterparts (Fuentes and Ehrenreich 1983:9; Snow 1979:27). Some researchers suggest that wages for female workers in these multinational firms are so low that subsistence can not be guaranteed (Wong 1981:451; Safa 1981:429; Frobel et al 1980: 359; Paglaban 1978:5).

There is evidence to suggest that the wages female workers earn in multinational concerns for their intensive labour are low, but it is appropriate to note that Malaysian women's wages in electronics factories are relatively low. Their wages are also linked to the organisation of work in Malaysia in terms of the nation state being connected to the world economic order which has caused the depression of labour[4] value through the mechanism of unequal exchange (see Arrighi 1972).

Yet, in contrast to other Southeast Asian countries and in comparison to female electronics workers in the United States, Malaysian women earn a medium level wage, while women in Singapore earn among the highest wages in Southeast Asia. Generally, Malaysian and Singaporean women earn a wage that is equal to male and female skilled workers in their country. In comparison to the average basic wage of electronics production workers in semiconductor multinationals in other Southeast Asian countries, Malaysian and Singaporean workers earn as a basic wage $.48 and .79 per hour compared to .53, .48 and .19 per hour with fringe/wage benefits $.60 and 1.25 compared to .80, .50 and .35 per hour respectively for Taiwan, the Philippines and Indonesia (Fuentes and Ehrenreich 1983: Semiconductor International 1982). Fringe and wage benefits are a regular, daily addition to the daily wage, especially after the apprenticeship period has been completed (Grossman 1979). The average wage level for all male and female workers in 1980 in Malaysia, Taiwan and the Philippines was $.28, .52 and .21 per hour (unskilled labourers) and $.62, .60 and .24 per hour (skilled labourers) respectively (Siegel 1981). In contrast in the United States a semiconductor assembler earns an average of $4.25-5.00 per hour (entry wages) to $5.50-7.50 per hour (experienced workers). A beginning wage refers to entry workers who have less than one year's experience, while an experienced worker has generally had two to four years experience on the job (Santa Clara County 1984). The figures demonstrate that the average female semiconductor worker in Malaysia earns as much if not more with wage/fringe benefits than the average skilled worker in her country and certainly more than the average unskilled labourer. Malaysian and Singaporean electronics assemblers earn less than their United States counterparts in 'Silicon Valley', but the fact that the cost of living in the United States is higher than in Malaysia and Singapore must be taken into account. In general, Malaysian female electronics workers earn above subsistence level wages with starting pay between U.S. $54.00-60.00 and after two years of employment, wages rising to U.S. $100.00 with monthly expenses of U.S. $45.00 (Grossman 1979:10). On average, the Malaysian electronics worker sends 25-50 per cent of her wages to her family in the village. However, in relation to the profits accrued to the multinational companies Malaysian women are paid low wages. It is estimated that an hour of work by an electronics worker in Malaysia produces enough profit to pay ten workers on a shift in addition to the costs of transport and materials (Grossman 1979:7). The lack of opportunities for promotion also serves to maintain a low wage level for electronics workers. One study, for example found that less than 3 per cent of 120 female electronics workers sampled were promoted in one Malaysian factory (Jamilah 1980b).

The wage of the Malaysian electronics worker is also basically low in the sense that her job is obtained at the expense of the remainder of her family members who are confined to eroding agrarian sectors. Both husbands and daughters attempt to find work in the urban areas, migrating to the cities and towns to obtain factory work. The possible participation however of a husband or daughter in the world market factory such as electronics is contingent upon the backwardness of the rural agrarian sector. The rural subsistence sector at the level of the community is linked to the world economic order through the nation state and provides without cost to the industrialised sector at the level of the nation state, the low cost reproduction of the labour force. In world market factories, employment is usually provided for one member of a rural family rather than all the adult members of the kinship unit. The wage however, is only high enough to support to a higher standard of living one person with some money to spare to contribute to remaining members of the family who can no longer survive solely from subsistence production. As women, daughters in particular, are preferred as workers in multinational firms, increasing numbers of rural Malaysian families because they are pressured by a declining agrarian sector that requires fewer labour intensive tasks, rely on the wages of their employed daughters. Daughters are the least essential members needed for family farming subsistence, as males traditionally work the field while mothers participate in some essential field work, raise the children and are largely responsible for domestic tasks (Strange 1981). Daughters do make a vital contribution to field work, domestic work and child rearing tasks, but they may be replaced by other siblings, extended family members or in some cases women belonging to the mutual aid network of the mothers. The employment of daughters by electronics factories therefore provides a welcome financial contribution to the survival of the family and their employment is either encouraged or tolerated by parents. Brothers and sisters who depend in part on the earnings of sisters for an education also encourage their participation in electronics production work.

The role of education

In Southeast Asian countries such as Malaysia and especially Singapore world market factories benefit from the higher educational levels attained by Asian females. Malaysian electronic plants require a high school education from production workers. The majority of of Malaysian female electronics workers have completed at least high school and have not worked previously for wages. A study of Penang, Malaysia found that two-thirds of the female electronics workers come from families in which they had not worked previously for wages. Some had hoped to obtain white-collar work or teaching positions, but none were available (Grossman 1979:8). These females were mainly daughters who had worked on family plots in rural areas for non-monetary rewards and were the most expendable members of the family (Strange 1981). Daughters from poorer households, although not under achievers at school are compelled by their household circumstances and the lack of alternative 'modern work' to work in world market factories. Government or other white-collar employment is often preferred by daughters, but without the appropriate connections in urban areas it is nearly impossible to obtain. Education is viewed as very important for both sons and daughters. Malaysian peasant women wish to educate their daughters so that they may obtain relatively high paying work, whether it is in world market factories or the government which will enable mothers to retire early. They desire ideally to retire from the fields at an early age, having their daughters provide for them in retirement and contribute to buying consumer goods for the home. Education in Malaysia has come to be associated with clean, better remunerated work and is linked to modern consumer goods acquisition which is becoming highly valued in the villages (McLellan 1985).

Educational attainment has been increasing for both men and women in Singapore along with ideas of greater value being attached to education. Education is viewed as a requisite for desirable employment opportunities and women for example who obtain a higher education at university are expected to become involved in professional employment. The costs and social expectations of the Singaporean middle classes are increasing which compels women with a high level of education to seek professional employment (Lim 1984:24). In the past two decades educational opportunities generally have been extended to the majority of the population. Primary education is free to all citizens. Female students constitute approximately half of those enrolled in primary, secondary and university levels of education. Many girls enter electronic assembly work because they are educated to a relatively high level, although fewer girls tend to elect for secondary technical education (Wong 1980:8). As noted previously women are already 'trained' for the delicate handling of materials having been socialised for domestic tasks. Therefore as production workers in the electronics factories, they mainly need a high enough level of education to read instructions and to follow directions properly. With the rise in manufacturing industry in the late sixties, early seventies, a decline in employment in the technical and professional fields occurred with women of all ethnic groups entering the manufacturing sector (Wong 1980:8-9). Although all ethnic groups including Chinese, Indian and Malay women entered the expanding manufacturing sector the rate and type of participation varied according to ethnic group. (See Table 2).[5]

Ethnic factors

The majority of Malaysian and Singaporean women who engage in electronics work are Malays. Although Chinese and Indian inhabitants of these islands are at the level of nationality Malaysian or Singaporean, on the level of their ethnic group they are Chinese and Indian. Chinese and Indian members of the community, have been absorbed into Malay culture to a limited extent and Malays are prejudiced in particular against the Chinese whom they view as dominating educational and occupational opportunities in the country (New Straits Times 1981). Chinese women were drawn originally into the early explanding manufacturing industries such as textiles, but left this sector for better paying white-collar jobs in the commercial sector in the seventies (See Table 2).[5]

Asian women are preferred in general for electronics production work because the delicate nature of the work requires patience and a willingness to work long, hard hours. Asian women in Southeast Asian countries are preferred by world market factories in particular because of a combination of factors that are located in the combination of modes specific to Southeast Asia. These factors which have been reviewed include the geographical location which gave rise to particular forms of agriculture that fostered an historical pattern of high female participation in this region. This factor occurred within the mode of ethnicity which gave rise to a nationality with its attendant ethnic peculiarities. The second factor is that of gender socialisation which 'trains' women through sex role differentiation for 'feminine occupations' and produces obedient females who are receptive to male authority. This occurs within the organisation of kinship which structures family relations and how children are socialised. The third factor is that of low wages and the attendant factor of education which are related to the organisation of work. The world economic order and its links to the nation and the community determine the availability of pools of cheap labour. Colonial intervention through the world economic order produced a semi-developed national infrastructure which included provisions for education. Education has spread throughout the community and has supplied a reasonably educated workforce for multinational firms that operate at the national level but are owned by companies located in advanced developing nations who operate them through the world economic order. These linked factors of combined modes produce particular effects which make Southeast Asian women preferred workers for multinational companies.

We have assessed the effects of Malaysian women's incorporation into world market factories in Malaysia and Singapore using the electronics industry as an example in terms of wages, conditions and education. Yet, this case study has mainly concentrated on the linkages and relations between these women workers at the level of the nation and world economic order. It is therefore apposite at this point to analyse the effects of these unique combination of modes in relation to women workers at the level of their communities, families and households, assessing the social and personal rather than the economic and political. (The combination modes theory is flexible in that it allows analysis of social change from the bottom up of the community household/level to the world economic order and down again).

Women electronics workers and change in relation to their families and communities

Despite the fact that it is the family role of the daughter which is most directly affected by the introduction of world market factories such as electronics, all family relations have been altered by the combined impact of multinational penetration at the levels of the world economic order and the nation state, and the subsequent reorganisation of labour. The emphasis on marriage for daughters, although remaining traditional in the majority of cases, has changed, in relation to poorer and middle income peasant rural families who have become dependent on the earnings of their female children in world market factories such as electronics Poorer families in particular often become so dependent on the earnings of their daughters for survival that they resist the desire of their female children to marry. Married daughters may constitute a threat to the survival of their families because their incomes may accrue to the families of their husbands. Both fathers and mothers in these cases exercise control over their daughters by pressuring them to remain unmarried, important financial contributors to family survival (Grossman 1979). The cultural idea that children must respect their parents and the debt the former owe the latter, especially mothers for having raised children is not only required by Islamic codes of behaviour but by Malayan tradition. Filial duty prescribes that children including daughters work, even if the mother does not require money urgently. Wealthier families continue to expect money to be sent from children as a sign of respect and honour, while poorer families not only desire the respect, but need the pecuniary contributions urgently. Daughters as major contributors to the financial welfare of the family has become an acceptable idea to families and the community in general.

In the case of a daughter failing to support her mother the latter is viewed by the community as not rearing her child properly. Mothers are proud of daughters who send them money and help them to make improvements in the house and to buy consumer goods. Mothers also encourage their daughters to work because it fosters the mothers' transition into the next socially desirable stage of the life cycle whereby they are supported by their children (McLellan 1985:10-11).

Even in the cases in which daughters are valued for their significant financial contribution and are not encouraged to marry, certain patriarchal kin relations remain intact which conflict with factory life. Daughters tend to be subject to the surveillance of kin, while brothers exercise relative freedom of movement. Females are considered responsible for the honour and shame attached to their families and are raised to be cautious concerning immodest behaviour. Female sexuality, for example, that is not confined to marriage is considered to be immodest behaviour that can bring shame upon the entire household. Divorce, however, is frequent because of the ease of divorce, and polygamy (McLellan 1985:12). Fathers and brothers are viewed as the protectors of the sexuality of their kinswomen until husbands assume this role upon marriage. Married women are expected to be obedient and behave modestly with their husbands. Yet, because of the strong bilineal historical kinship patterns that continue to be practised with women managing the household, serving as treasurers and being allowed to earn their own money women are both responsible and independent members of the family. Women also need to be independent and to be able to manage financial affairs because of the preponderance of divorce. Daughters are raised to be industrious and in their late teens are capable of managing the household and often earn money as basket or mat weavers or agricultural labourers (McLellan 1985: Strange 1981). The responsible, independent actions expected of women by rural Malaysian families facilitate their entrance into electronics factory work, but the lack of emphasis on modest behaviour within the factories is a source of tension between the family and the working daughter or wife.

As tensions exist between the modest behaviour expected of daughters and their responsible, independent upbringing, work in electronics factories away from home exacerbates such contradictions. Electronics workers experience a degree of independence unknown to their female relations remaining in the villages. Women workers may visit friends late at night, have boyfriends, wear makeup and Western dress without being subject to the guarded 'protection' of fathers and brothers (Grossman 1979). Fathers and brothers experience a sense of loss of control over daughters and sisters and a feeling of inadequacy in relation to guarding the chastity of female kin, especially in the case of daughters migrating to the urban areas outside the village. These tensions are intensified in the cases of daughters or sisters who return to their village to visit, expressing their new independence quite blatantly in wearing make-up or tight jeans and exhibiting Western cultural manners that are promoted by the electronics firms for whom they work. Parents and brothers in particular often complain to electronics companies about the new independent lifestyles that their daughters or sisters have adopted while living alone in the towns or company hostels. Some companies seek to allay the fears of kin members by providing factory-owned hostels that are supervised by chaperones and practice strict rules regarding visitors to the hostels and visits made outside by employees (Grossman 1970). Some factories use buses to collect and deliver female workers to and from electronics factories. In providing such transportation factories may widen their labour pool, pay lower wages and argue that it reduces chances of daughters engaging in misbehaviour. Old men are often used as security guards and bus drivers to reassure parents, and factory managers provide parents with assurances concerning their daughters' moral welfare. A number of factories invite parents for factory visits or 'family days' where village leaders and parents are provided with a traditional feast which utilises cultural values of food and reciprocity to encourage parents to send their daughters to work in world market factories such as electronics. Some managers prefer the female workers to live in their villages under the control of village leaders and parents because it makes them more compliant as they have not been separated from the village regimen. The female workers who are bussed to work are usually from the poorest families and are paid less because they remain part of their household. Daughters that commute independently or who live outside the village in urban areas or EPZ's are paid the highest wages and are the object of sensational journalism which portrays them as 'loose' and 'immoral' (McLellan 1986:6-7). This latter group faces the greatest amount of tension because of the extent of their break with tradition.

Despite the fact that many electronics companies attempt to dispel the fears of family members their presence and practices heighten tensions within the kin unit and for female workers. Brothers feel resentment for employed sisters when they are unable to obtain work because electronics firms for example prefer female employees. Fathers experience tension as well, especially in the case of declining subsistence agriculture displacing them from their role as major providers for the family and may feel great resentment toward daughters who are contributing as much or more than they are able towards the survival of the family. Family members may feel resentment toward a married daughter (this occurs more frequently in the Singaporean case) who contributes her earnings to her immediate nuclear family, but who requires assistance with child care, as few electronics factories provide creche facilities (Wong 1980). Daughters or wives need the emotional and perhaps in future financial support of their families, yet they desire the freedom, earnings and independence that the factory life offers.

The particular manner in which the modes of the organisation of work, kinship and ethnicity have combined in Malaysia and Singapore produces on the community level tensions between female electronics workers, kin members and village members because they are torn between different desires and needs, traditions and modernities. In the event that influences from the levels of the world economic order and nation state cause the expansion of world market factories such as electronics, affecting the organisation of work and kinship, such tensions will most likely increase leading perhaps to a more fundamental shift in social ideology among the indigenous Malays.

We have been using women as a vehicle of analysis within the context of combination modes theory which have served to explain the mechanisms of social change in relation to a Southeast Asian nation developing along capitalist lines. It is also clear that the modes of organisation most directly affected by such social change are those of the organisation of work and kinship. Chapter three will focus on a small isolated socialist experiment - the Kibbutz - which continues to thrive as a socioeconomic entity within the capitalist Israeli context. The combination modes thesis will be applied to the analysis of the changing position of women within the Kibbutz system showing how social change may be initiated from the bottom up unlike the Malaysian case. The organisation of ethnicity and kinship will have greater focus in this case study.

Notes

1. There have been moves towards replacing Silicon as the basic component of chip manufacture with a new material gallium arsenide (Ga As). The United States military which initiated the development of the new wafer substance is currently investing less in this type of research because of the high cost of Ga As. A four inch blank wafer of Ga As costs $3,000 compared to $200 for a six inch Silicon wafer (Global Electronics 1988:1).

2. See the statistics compiled by the International Labour Organisation (Asian Employment Programme 1980) which show a stabilisation in women's participation in rural work and increased numbers of rural females entering the total workforce after multinational investment occurred in 1972.

3. Table one. Employed females by selected occupations in which there were more than 10,000 female workers, 1978. (See page 66).

4. However, connections with the world economic order has also initiated a valuing of labour power with the end in September 1988 of Malaysian electronics industries ban on unions. The lifting of the government ban was in response to petitioning from the American AFL-CIO (Global Electronics 1988:4).

5. Table 2. Working/employed females by industry and ethnic groups 1957-1978. (See page 67).

TABLE ONE

Employed females by selected occupations in which there were more than 10,000 female workers, 1978

Selected occupations	Total Persons	Female	% Female
Teachers	20,608	11,915	57.8
Stenographers, typists, card-and-tape punching machine operators	14,608	13,463	92.2
Bookkeepers, financial record clerks, cashiers & related workers	27,159	17,258	63.5
Clerical and related workers not elsewhere classified	70,707	39,605	56.0
Salesmen, shop assistants and related workers	101,640	35,597	35.0
Domestic service workers	15,435	15,032	97.4
Tailors, dressmakers, sewers, upholsterers and related workers	27,308	23,110	84.6
Electrical fitters and related electrical and electronics workers	58,156	40,368	69.4

Source: Labour Force Survey of Singapore, 1978

TABLE TWO

Working/employed females by industry and ethnic group 1957-1978

Industry	1957 Chinese	1957 Malays	1957 Indians	1970 Chinese	1970 Malays	1970 Indians	1978 Chinese	1978 Malays	1978 Indians
Agriculture, forestry & fishing	12.5	8.1	2.8	3.4	1.0	0.3	1.7	0.5	0.6
Mining & quarrying	0.2	-	-	0.1	-	0.1	-	-	0.3
Manufacturing	21.0	3.7	2.1	32.2	31.2	18.9	36.1	55.3	43.5
Electricity, gas and water	0.1	0.1	0.6	0.4	0.2	0.6	0.3	0.8	0.8
Construction	2.2	0.3	1.2	2.0	0.2	0.8	1.9	0.5	1.3
Commerce	16.0	10.9	8.5	19.6	11.8	12.8	26.5	10.9	12.9
Transport and communication	1.0	0.5	2.3	2.4	3.1	3.2	4.7	5.8	6.6
Finance, insurance and business services	2.3	0.6	1.7	3.6	0.9	2.3	8.4	5.8	6.4
Community, social and personal services	44.5	75.7	80.4	36.2	51.6	60.9	20.4	20.4	27.6
Activities not adequately defined	0.2	0.1	0.4	0.1	-	0.1	-	-	-
Total	100.0 76,217	100.0 3,438	100.0 1,441	100.0 136,489	100.0 9,737	100.0 4,475	100.0 250,200	100.0 44,608	100.0 17.491

Source: Wong 1980.

2 The Kibbutz: collective led cooperatives

The Kibbutz experiment provides us with an example of a society that has made a radical departure from previously known societies. The three combination modes of the organisation of work, kinship and ethnicity have all been organised in a unique manner that has challenged traditional patriarchal or matriarchal societies and has attempted to create an egalitarian bilineal society. This egalitarian organisation of kinship has been created within a socialist organisation of work and within a strictly Jewish organisation of ethnicity. The many roles of women within the Kibbutz movement have been seen generally during the pioneering generation as revolutionising the definition of gender and gender roles. Rosner and Palgi argue (1980:12) that the Kibbutz has fostered some of the most egalitarian interpersonal relationships based on partnership and equal abilities stressed between the sexes, which is reflected in the none stereotypical partnership experienced at the micro-level of the family. However, a noticeable trend has been emerging among Kibbutz women, especially among the generations furthest removed from the pioneers towards familism and an even further marginalisation in their public roles within the Kibbutz system. The reasons for this occurrence may be explained historically within the context of combination modes and how they have altered since the inception of the Kibbutz movement. Variations also exist according to the Kibbutz groups (i.e. Artzi or Ichud) under scrutiny.

Theoretical arguments relating to women and familism

Contemporary theorists and researchers of Kibbutz life, puzzled by the apparent rejection of gender equality by women have suggested a number of determining factors that seek to explain the recent intensive interest of the female Sabra Kibbutz members in the family. A number of theories have emerged to further understanding of this tendency. Some theorists view as inevitable women's recurring interest in the family because of biological reasons and womens' 'natural' maternal instincts (i.e. Spiro 1980; Irvine 1980; Tiger and Shepher (1975). Other theorists suggest that social determining factors are the cause of renewed interest in family life among women on the Kibbutz (i.e. Gerson 1978, 1974; Hurwitz 1965; Bettelheim 1969). Bettelheim (1969) argues from a more social but also biological perspective that increasing familial tendencies are a form of protest against masculine unmotherly behaviour of their own mothers of the pioneering generation. Talmon (1972) found in her studies that a link exists between the degree of satisfaction achieved by women in their public roles and the extent to which they favour more familistic arrangements on the Kibbutz. She found for example that professional women are less inclined to support family rather than collective sleeping arrangements. Others suggest that the masculine pattern of behaviour was established during the pioneering period because of the emphasis on physical strength, introducing women to masculine roles, while retaining feminine ones as inferior (Mednick 1975; Keller 1973). Rosner and Palgi (1980) on the other hand suggest, that women's familistic tendencies must be viewed in the context of a general move towards the lessening of the collective framework of the Kibbutz and the move towards individualism. All these theories hold a degree of efficacy when viewed within the context of the historical changes that have taken place according to the modes of the organisation of work, kinship and ethnicity since the inception of the Kibbutz system. These combined changes have resulted in an internal shift in social ideology towards greater individualism and familistic tendencies.

Historical development of the Kibbutz system

The Kibbutz movement cannot be separated from the historical process that inspired it. The roots of the movement lay within the organisation of ethnicity at the level of the ethnic group who were the Jewish people in this case. The impetus for the movement was the desire of the Jewish people to return to their ancient homeland of Israel (Zion) from which they had been displaced two thousand years before (the Diaspora) and was kindled by the national liberation movements that were occurring throughout the Western and Eastern European communities of the late nineteenth century. The Jewish population forced to live in the outskirts of large towns in Russia, Poland, Galicia, and Romania, the Pale of Settlement, were the subject of savage attacks from the frustrated Russian peasantry and emergent lower middle class. The remaining feudal order was in decay and the feudal landlord and aristocratic Romanoffs utilised the easily identifiable Jew as scapegoat (Leon 1970:226-228). Two possible solutions emerged for the Jews of Eastern Europe who became impoverished and under seige. One, was emigration to other countries such as Britain or the United States and the other was to return or make 'Aliyah' to what was then called Palestine. The first wave of immigration to Palestine occurred between 1880-95, the second from 1905-14 and the third aliyah between 1919-25. The future members of the Kibbutz began to arrive with the second Aliyah and were derived from the town dwelling Jewish population who had left the villages when the emergence of industrialism had led to a general reformation for the peasantry which lessened restriction on the Jews. These young Eastern European immigrants to Palestine had mixed with the Russian intelligensia, and broadened their political outlook, encompassing socialist, liberal and communist thought. They combined these ideas with the establishment of a new society in their ancient homeland. The youths were mainly in their teens and twenties.

In 1910, the first Kibbutz or collective establishment Degania, was established. The third aliyah, which was greatly influenced by the Russian revolution, brought with them radical, revolutionary social ideology. These immigrants established Kibbutzim that pooled resources and they attempted to form personal collective relationships rather than individualistic ones. They also attempted to close the gap in social differences made between skilled and unskilled labour (Gerson 1978:3-5).

The early Kibbutz members shared their youth, enthusiasm, ideals and a resolve to transform their diaspora mentality. They sought to accomplish these common goals by returning to a life of farming and self-sufficiency which was a way of life that had been denied them in Eastern Europe. The youths desired to become once again close to nature, physically productive and free of the corrupting culture of urban life.

Physical labour, construction, industrial and farm labour, which had been associated with low status occupations in their countries of origin became labour of high status, while business and commerce which they viewed as exploitative careerist activities became labour of low status (Spiro 1980:10).

The Kibbutz movement at its inception attempted to establish a radical reorganisation of the modes of work and kinship within the context of a Jewish organisation of ethnicity. It attempted to extricate itself from the world economic order, the Kibbutzniks countries' of origin and Palestine as an Arab nation state, transforming the organisation of work to a fully socialist form, integrating women into the 'productive' work process. The family was transformed from a socioeconomic unit of production, with the allocation and distribution of wealth taking place on a collective basis. Individual members received shares of collective earnings according to need, which made lines of descent, title and inheritance irrelevant to the survival of the Kibbutz household. Children (when the Kibbutzim felt they were economically viable enough to have children) lived separately from their parents and authority has been hypothetically a function of all the members of the collective. Domestic and reproductive tasks were socialised through communal infant care, eating facilities and cleaning services. The young pioneers were also determined to change the organisation of kinship through alterations in the sexual division of labour according to the sexes.

Members of the early Kibbutzim believed in an ideology that rejected the subjection of women and children to the power of the father within the family. Paternal domination in the family embodied Jewish shtetl life and that of those Jewish families living in European cities. The majority of females who were immigrants to Palestine did not possess a particularly formalised ideology of woman's emancipation, although they were sensitive to aspects of the oppression of women. Nevertheless, young pioneer women were most enthusiastic about the task that lay before them and they wanted to engage in productive work (Rein 1980:27-28).

The historical exclusion of pioneer women from productive work in the earliest Kibbutzim

Several obstacles, however, arose to the active participation of women even from the earliest days of the Kibbutzim.

For both economical and ideological reasons, traditional female domestic tasks were not regarded as productive work. Agricultural labour or guard duty, typically male tasks, were the ones imbued with the status of productive work (Gerson 1978:33-34). This was despite the fact that education and domestic service tasks such as childrearing, were instrumental in shaping the lives of future generations of Kibbutz members, who would be the guardians of collective socialist ideology. Women were encouraged to enter spheres of male work and political activity to create a more equal sexual division of labour for both men and women, but men were not encouraged to enter the work sectors of women. The emphasis during the pioneer period was on physical strength, which supported the masculine pattern of work (Mednick 1975; Keller 1973).

From the earliest days of the establishment of the Kibbutzim women were not allowed in large numbers into male spheres of production and they had to fight resolutely to enter agriculture or construction. Even after struggling to enter male spheres of labour, not more than 11 per cent of men from the inception of the Kibbutz movement worked in traditional female spheres of labour on a temporary basis (Gerson 1978:34). Therefore, despite the desire to implement an egalitarian division of labour in relation to the sexes, such attempts were not successful from the beginning of the settlements.

Additionally, the majority of the founding members of the early Kibbutzim were male bachelors. The founders of the first Kibbutz in 1911, Degania, consisted of twelve young Russian Jews - ten male and two female (Gerson 1978:4). The bulk of young childless immigrants were men, with males often outnumbering females four or five to one (Hecht and Davis 1979:100). This disproportionate sex ratio occurred because the leaders of the Zionist movement in Europe, who were males that bought and owned land in Palestine, did not encourage women to immigrate. Although small numbers of women were sponsored to immigrate by their Zionist groups; upon reaching Palestine they were separated from the men and were relegated to service tasks under the employment of men (Katznelson-Rubashow 1932:182). A number of collectives did not have women as full-time members but only hired women to perform domestic tasks, while others refused to accept more than the limited number of women needed to provide services (Maimon undated).

It was difficult for women to sustain a consistent struggle for the chance to engage in productive labour that held equal status to men through discussion and pressurisation of male members, because the environmental conditions were so harsh (Laquer 1972:80). Most of the energies of the young pioneers were spent on survival and rebuilding the land, rather than adhering strictly to an ideology that had been formulated in the Eastern European youth movements. The preoccupation with daily survival intensified when pregnancies occurred and the need for childcare arose. Pregnant women who had worked in agriculture became increasingly removed from production as confinement and the need for childcare developed. Many mothers breastfeeding their babies were required to move into service work sectors to be in closer proximity to the infants' house. As the number of children multiplied an accompanying need for service workers increased and because a sexual division of labour that was close to traditional European society was being established, it was women who were drawn from farm labour into the communal services (Spiro 1980:16).

Finally, any work that was available was given to male members of the collective. Men were given priority in farm work because it was argued that pregnancies made women an irregular feature of any workforce and that because women received lower wages than men, the former's contribution to the collective would be reduced. Another economic argument proposed that it was illogical for women to work in male sectors when they could earn money performing feminine work. To relieve female unemployment, a few of the settlements established restaurants and launderettes to serve group members working in the cities. In other collective groups, women worked outside the Kibbutzim, as paid domestic labourers so that they were able to contribute to the common held resources.

Therefore, despite the desire of the pioneers of the Kibbutz movement to challenge and reorganise in a fundamental manner kinship and work organisation in relation to the sexual division of labour, this process was impeded by a combination of historical and culturally traditional reasons. Women were never fully incorporated into productive labour and men were never encouraged to enter child orientated educational or service occupations. Although the family as a socioeconomic unit had been abolished along with the authority role of individual families, women tended to remain collectively in traditional family oriented services. Children's education and collective services have gained in status since the pioneer days, but such branches continue to have less status attached to them because no income is derived from these sectors (Rosner and Palgi 1980:25). The composition therefore of the particular combination modes during the early days of the Kibbutz movement laid the foundations for future changes in the position of women and their move towards familism, self-realisation and social affiliation.

The move towards increased familism

Contemporary research has found that despite the abolition of the economic base of capitalism and the fostering of some of the most egalitarian interpersonal relationships based on partnership and equal abilities stressed between the sexes (Rosner and Palgi 1980:12), women of the younger generation (Sabra) are turning to traditional social roles (Spiro 1980; Rosner and Palgi 1980; Irvine 1980; Gerson 1978; Tiger and Shepher 1975; Gerson 1974; Alon 1970; Bettleheim 1969; Rosner 1967; Hurwitz 1965).

Women who are located mainly in service sectors dealing with domestic collective, children's educational arrangements are actively pursuing traditional female preoccupations typical to Western industrialised society such as the emphasis on outward appearances and the desire to re-establish the individual family household as a unit of consumption and authority. The recent trends differ markedly from the early days of the Kibbutz system when female settlers (pioneers) fought for equality with their male counterparts in all spheres of endeavour. The Sabra female descendants of the early collectives do not wish to follow the precedents set by their grandmothers and strive to be involved in female pursuits traditional to patriarchal societies, such as the family, beauty, children and decorating the home. Women are spending more of their allocated income and time in the home, on furnishings for the home and aspects of individual childcare. They are also making increased demands for the equal distribution of collective monies as the distribution of money takes the form of the direct supply of goods and services according to need on a legitimate basis to individuals and families. The majority of women on the Kibbutzim tend to support the idea of the distribution of equal amounts of money so that each person or family may decide where and what is to be bought for consumption purposes (Rosner 1986).

Recent research has shown that involvement with the family has become a major concern for many second generation native born Kibbutz women. In 1975, a public opinion survey asked members of Kibbutz Artzi, which is the most socialised sector of the Kibbutz movement, to rank in order of importance the following activities; work, family, study, hobbies and public activities. The majority of female members placed the family at the top of their list of priorities, while the bulk of male respondents ranked work as their most important concern (Leviatan 1975:23). A generational study of a non-Kibbutz Artzi collective found that 32 per cent of men compared to 68 per cent of women of the pioneering generation considered their role as worker to be less important than of spouse and parent. With regard to the second generation the gap in percentages widened with 27 per cent of men compared to 88 per cent of women, believing their roles as workers to be less important than their family roles (Shain 1974:174-75, 208-9).

In recent years, the majority of young married women on many of the Kibbutzim have become actively committed to housewife and mothering roles; for example baking cakes, knitting or crocheting sweaters and preparing the evening meal on the Sabbath for the family (Spiro 1980:32). Sabra women have tended to have more children than their predecessors, partly because the current economic prosperity permits the collectives to support 'non-productive' child members, viewing childcare as a natural, important part of personal fulfillment, marrying earlier, and generally investing heavily in the family. The number of births has been rising steadily since the Sixties and is at least 4 percentage points higher than the birth-rate of the Jewish population in Israel as a whole (Rosner and Palgi 1980:5). Recently, it has been easier for women in the Kibbutz system to acquire professional as well as vocational training and some prospective mothers postpone bearing children until they have completed their education. However, once young women bear children they are reluctant to study away from the Kibbutz and their infants, which was not an unusual practice in earlier years. Sabra women are tending to resent any interference with their family life (Gerson 1978:37; Irvine 1980:25).

The majority of women of the pioneering generation are disapproving of the family-centred attitudes of many young Sabra women, viewing them as retreating from the outside world into traditional housewifely pursuits (Spiro 1980:32). The second generation of women born on the Kibbutzim, express quite openly without ideological restraint their preference for a greater feminine role which is similar to the Western female stereotype of woman as wife, mother and beauty object. Young Kibbutz men as well as older pioneer men, tend to support the contention of younger women that their primary role is that of wife and mother (Alon 1970:292). Younger women unlike their pioneer grandmothers do not insist on performing 'men's' work but rather accept female service and educational work.

A trend has been noted for women to retreat into family isolation in their individual apartments by a researcher who found '... exaggerated interest in improving the room, withdrawal from the life of the communiity, absence from general meetings' (Hurwitz 1965:357). Kibbutz members in many of the collectives are no longer required to utilise standard Kibbutz furniture and the recent pre-occupation of women with interior design of the residences has been facilitated by a cash allowance for furniture (Spiro 1980:43). This trend towards familism has tended to parallel a move in the direction of individualism and the expansion of the family sphere in which women find primary expression (Rosner and Palgi 1980:31-32). Women also emphasise social attachments and the need for affiliation, while men emphasise achievement and guiding the course of Kibbutz life. Men stress as well the attainment of national and socialistic goals, while women emphasise self-realisation and social values (Rosner and Palgi 1980:34,40). Women are having a greater involvement in matters related to appearance and are adopting a Western form of feminine identity through the wearing of feminine dress and accoutrements such as cosmetics, perfumes, coiffed hair and jewellery (Rosner and Palgi 1980:34; Spiro 1980:42; Gerson 1978:292).

Perhaps one of the most profound alterations in both attitude as well as practice from pioneer days to the present concerns the change in young Sabra women's ideas about preparing the child for sleep (hashkava) and a desire to turn collective sleeping (lina meshutefet) into family sleeping (lina mispachtit). The latter refers to children sleeping privately in the quarters of their parents. Nurses in the children's house from the beginning of the collectivisation of housework had prepared all the Kibbutz children for bed, but because of maternal pressure in recent years, parents have assumed this responsibility.

Collective sleeping in the children's house which has been deemed an essential part of Kibbutz ideology from its inception is meeting with increased demands for change. In a six-Kibbutz survey conducted in 1975, it was found that 55 per cent of native born young women preferred family, while 27 per cent preferred collective sleeping arrangements and 21 per cent were undecided (Spiro 1980:35). The majority of Kibbutzim, those with the strongest commitment to the founding ideology such as the Kibbutz Artzi Federation have resisted such a fundamental change in their systems. However, three-fourths of the Ichud Kibbutz Federation which has the weakest ideological commitment has succumbed to internal pressure and instituted family sleeping (Spiro 1980:35; Rosner and Palgi 1980:14). Many Kibbutz members, especially those of the pioneer generation, view the family sleeping arrangement with disdain, believing that it may undermine commitment to the collective ideology. Ironically, sexual equality has been more readily attained within the micro-structure of the family rather than the macro-structure of the Kibbutz. Husbands in the study by Tiger and Shepher (1975) were seen to contribute heavily to domestic work within the household, with only 4 out of 13 household tasks performed solely by the adult women of the household. The four tasks included bringing foodstuffs, preparing the afternoon meal, cleaning the kitchenette and the bathroom, while other jobs such as cleaning the flat or washing the dishes was performed by both partners alternatively or together (Rosner and Palgi 1980:10). Men's participation in housework becomes even greater in the case of large families and children sleeping at home. Rosner and Palgi (1980:11) argue that the role of men has become revolutionised in relation to the family with men invading areas of solidarity and emotionalism.[1] Women's roles in turn have not changed and have become further marginalised, while men's have widened. The organisation of kinship has been changing discernibly from one that was collectively based at the level of the lineage and community within the organisation of kinship and work respectively. Where increased emphasis on familism is occurring the organisation of kinship is shifting to the level of the extended family and the household. At the level of the community, the Kibbutz system has been increasing its links to the nation state and world economic order, especially since industrialisation has occurred on the Kibbutzim. The fact that the Kibbutz is a Jewish cultural community is the third component which combines to make the present day Kibbutz movement peculiar to itself. The Kibbutz as a cultural community contains intra-ethnic divisions between the Ashkenazi and the Sephardi who are Diaspora Jews returned from Western and Eastern parts of the world respectively. A review of the arguments of a number of theorists previously mentioned incorporate explanations for the trends towards familism that both support and challenge the combination modes thesis. These theories will be reviewed and criticised within the context of the combination modes argument.

Nature vs nurture vs socioeconomic organisation vs external factors?

A noteworthy study of Kibbutz women by Tiger and Shepher argues that a basic source of inequality between the sexes has been eliminated on the collectives through the abolition of the economic base of capitalist social organisation. They acknowledge that male dominated society in general does have an impact on the inferior status of women (Tiger and Shepher 1975:266), but argue strongly that the Kibbutz in its education system and every facet of its social organisation avoids sex-typing, thereby providing ideal conditions for full sexual equality. They also argue that women are slightly more limited than males in job choice. External influences from sources such as the world economic order and Israeli nation state are not taken into account in their analysis because it is maintained that the Kibbutzim have always been independent of Israel as a whole and that any contacts Kibbutz members do have with outsiders are of minimal importance. Therefore, it is maintained that under such ideal conditions of sexual equality, the only conceivable reason that Sabra women seek greater family involvement is because of their 'biogrammar'. Biogrammar is a genetic tendency in the human species which programmes a strong maternal relationship between a mother and her children. The Kibbutz system has tampered with nature by attempting to institute unnatural female roles and the suppression of female instinct. The rebellion of second generation women is a result of an unnatural order promoted by the collectives. The biological based argument of the human nature thesis in relation to the changing position of women on the Kibbutz has been supported by theorists such as Irvine (1980).

Irvine (1980) argues that the pioneers understandably failed to internalise the ideology of sex equality to which they subscribed because they were influenced by their pre-pioneering social conditioning. This fact she suggests does not explain why the second generation of Kibbutzniks, who have been raised entirely in the 'correct' social conditions are more, not less attached to the idea of the family. The latter point is seen as convincing evidence that human nature, which is resistant to interference has re-established itself (Irvine 1980:29).

The biological argument presented by these theorists is relevant in the sense that because of women's biological reproductive capacity females were required to move away from farm work to nurse their children. The early Kibbutzim discouraged childbearing because of the lack of available resources. The number of children multiplied along with increasing prosperity and women who had worked in agriculture became removed from production as the need for childcare developed. Many breastfeeding mothers were required to move into service work sectors to be in closer proximity to the infants' houses and because the sexual division of labour had already been established, it was women who were drawn from farm work into the communal services (Spiro 1980:16). Therefore biology in relation to the organisation of kinship had a role in drawing pioneer women and subsequent generations into family oriented service and domestic work away from statusful 'productive' labour. Yet, this argument is weak in relation to its human nature thesis and ideas of a 'natural' return of the mother to her biological duties, because it does not take into account external or historical factors. Rosner and Palgi (1980:9) note that the Kibbutz as a sub-sector of the larger society cannot insulate itself from such influences even when the social ideology of the greater Israeli society is contrary to egalitarian and socialistic values. They argue (1980:17) that the main problem does not reside within the economic sphere, but in the realm of culture and in the ability of the Kibbutz system to maintain its autonomy and identity within the context of the capitalist system. The ability of the Kibbutz system to maintain its autonomous belief system depends on whether its values are used to guide everyday life and activities which are implemented in social reality. This commitment to the collective ideology may be weakening generally as Rosner and Palgi (1980:14) note that women's familistic tendencies may be viewed in the context of a general move towards lessening of the collective framework and the strengthening of individual families. Tiger and Shepher therefore miss the importance of the linkages between the Kibbutz community, nation state and world economic order within the organisation of work that influence the tendencies of women towards familisim. Tiger and Shepher and Irvine overestimate the level of sexual equality reached in the Kibbutz system.

As the previous historical analysis shows, women were not absorbed equally into production and as Rosner and Palgi (1980:10-11) note, the egalitarian ideology of sexual equality is more efficient at the level of the micro-structure of the family rather than the macro-structure of the Kibbutz. Additionally, during the early days of the settlements, which constituted the foundation for future practice, sex equality in terms of members of both gender groups participating in precisely the same activities, was not a normative feature of Kibbutz life. (The reasons for this have been outlined in the section of this chapter dealing with the ways in which pioneer women were excluded from productive work).

A related interpretation of the human nature perspective is presented by Spiro (1980) who points to the distinction between the identity meaning of equality and the equivalent meaning of equality. He defines the former in terms of people being equal if they are identifical in one or more criterial attributes, while the equivalent meaning refers to different criterial attributes of people having the same worth.

He argues that the pioneers upheld the identity meaning of equality, which was impossible to achieve because pre-cultural conditions predicated on biology necessitated a difference in male and female roles. The increasing involvement of females with the family coupled with distinct feminine roles is seen by Spiro as a natural shift from the unobtainable identity equality to the more realistic equivalent equality. Spiro, therefore, does not interpret the behaviour of young females in terms of a reaction against their position in the Kibbutz because he believes the Kibbutz movement continues to practice and uphold equivalent equality (Spiro 1980: 59-60).

Spiro notes that for female Kibbutzniks, who are among the most educated women in Israel, confinement to the communalised service sectors may produce frustration with such repetitive chores. He argues, however, that women are not frustrated and bored because of the existence of the sexual division of labour, but experience ennui because rather than offering a wide variety of female occupations such as retail selling and nursing, the collectives provide women with a limited choice of domestic service tasks. He suggests that housewives in privatised spheres lead a more interesting life because they engage in a number of household based labours, while women on the Kibbutzim are confined to one chore for a prolonged period of time (Spiro 1980:56-58).

A survey that Spiro conducted found that the economic committees and secretariat, which are the main policy making bodies that present issues for the entire Kibbutz membership to decide upon, are comprised primarily of males. This disproportionate balance of power in favour of male membership is not viewed by him as a consequence of gender inequality. Rather, this situation demonstrates to Spiro that '... since by their own desires few women work in the agricultural and industrial branches of the Kibbutz economy, they typically have neither the experience nor the interest to deal with these matters' (Spiro 1980:59).

Spiro cites in his study similar practices on the Kibbutz which a great many theorists irrespective of their persuasion would find indicative of differential and lower status for women. Yet, he does not acknowledge such gender based inequality because he argues that women of the Kibbutz having been given complete freedom of choice are choosing (and some Sabra women have stated this in interviews) to engage in feminine occupations and behaviour. He substantiates his case through interviews with male and female Sabras in a six Kibbutz sample. The interviewees state that sexual social role differentiation is a reflection of biological differences in needs and interests, rather than in ability, talent, intellectual capacity, worth as human beings or the contribution made to Kibbutz society (Spiro 1980:60).

With reference to the historical portion of this chapter, neither identity nor equivalent equality as defined by Spiro was practicsed on the Kibbutz during the pioneering period. The priority of the early Kibbutz movement was not gender equality but a social ideology that emanated from a socialist organisation of the mode of work and a Jewish organisation of the mode of ethnicity. Jewish pioneers who formed the Kibbutzim sought to prove that Diaspora Jews were capable of succeeding in hard physical agricultural work and that socialistic collective farming can be an economically viable enteprise. Therefore, hard physical labour and productive work which generated income were given the greatest prestige, while services that did not generate an income and in which the majority of women worked, held a lesser status. Education, however, was an exception within this general tendency because of the traditional Jewish cultural emphasis on education and the high value placed on children (Rosner and Palgi 1980:27). Only a skewed form of identity equality occurred in that pioneer women who could meet the rigorous demands of hard physical labour in the overwhelmingly male productive sectors could share some form of identity equality with male counterparts. The organisation of work was socialised in that women were drawn into the labour force en masse with all female members incorporated into the work schedule as members of the labour force and providers for the collective welfare. Yet, a sexual division of labour with particular social ideological values had been instituted from the inception of the collectives, which placed women within the fields of education and services. Income was not derived from either sector and work in the services held low status. Although the work was socialised in that such services were part of the collective income, performed in public places and not for the family unit; the service sectors were consumption oriented, while the productive work emphasised professionalism and cost effectiveness because the products were sold on the market place(Rosner and Palgi 180:25). Identity equality is therefore an irrelevant concept in relation to the pioneer days because it was never implemented fully or established in the social ideology.

Equivalent equality as shown in the early history of the settlements did not exist because the priorities of hard physical labour and economic effectiveness did not allow women's service sector work to have as great a status as male dominated productive labour. Neither did the majority of women enjoy as great self-esteem, influence or self-fulfillment in relation to the professed social ideology of the Kibbutz movement as did their male counterparts. A form of equivalent equality in relation to the branches in which the majority of women work has been only a historically recent phenomenon. In the late seventies and early eighties with greater affluence occurring within the Kibbutz system and the general dissatisfaction of many women, significant investments have been made to improve conditions in the service sectors. Opportunities for the majority of women in the service sectors to gain professional degrees and experience increased substantially, with women in the services and education holding higher qualifications than men in the masculine branches (Rosner and Palgi 1980:27). Yet, equivalent equality is only a useful concept in the case of all members being given the same opportunity to utilise their potentials and this is a moot point, as the problem of sex-role polarisation continues to exist and perhaps is becoming more firmly entrenched. Rosner and Palgi's (1980) assessment of the importance of women's sex-role polarisation to women's dissatisfaction and which may be applied to understand moves towards familism, challenges Spiro's argument that women require a greater variety of service tasks to achieve their potentials.

Rosner and Palgi (1980:27-28) note that because of such polarisations, women are compelled to work in sectors that may be incompatible with their personal inclinations. Men also experience this problem because of the small size of the Kibbutz but to a lesser extent than for women. The potential achievement of adolescent girls may be curtailed because they see their mother's generation in a small number of 'feminine' occupations, which might interfere with their pursuit of disciplines deemed not essential for females. Occupational polarisation is also related to polarisation in the field of public roles which affects women's future economic participation in important positions such as the Kibbutz administration.

This has a related impact of women not attending Kibbutz general assemblies which lends itself to general apathy among women and a feeling that they are marginal members of the community. The fact that goods and supplies are distributed according to need through officeholders also puts women at a disadvantage in the area of distribution of goods as they are rarely officeholders or attend meetings to influence those in administrative positions. Occupational role flexibility is hindered as well as women are not prepared to deal with emergency situations in which they are required to replace absent male members (Rosner 1986).

The result of occupational polarisation therefore, is that women exert less influence in public spheres and are less likely to exercise their personal aspirations and inclinations. This tendency is reflected in differences between men and women in relation to the articulation of their life goals. Women stress social attachments, the need for affiliation, self-realisation and social values, while men emphasise achievement, national and socialistiic goals and guidance of the course of Kibbutz life (Rosner and Palgi 1980:34,40). As Kibbutz women are now among the most educated women in Israel, it is ironic that they continue to emphasise the need for self-realisation in their lives. If professionalising the education and service sectors does not meet the needs of womens' goal for self-realisation and they continue to demand a greater emphasis on the family, diversifying service sector tasks would most likely prove to be an unsatisfactory attempt to deal with this tendency.

In emphasising biological based differences and needs between men and women on the Kibbutz, Spiro underrates the importance of the historical factors that have shaped the present generation of female Kibbutz members. As the historical evidence shows, women of the pioneer generation were subject to a polarised sexual division of labour within the socialist organisation of work from the inception of the Kibbutz movement. Women of the second generation have been raised under conditions of sex-role occupational polarisation and a lower, marginalised status accorded to female work. Such alienation from what is defined as productive work I would argue, given the evidence, is linked to general female disinterest in the economic and administrative functions of the Kibbutzim as well as their withdrawal from the community.

Confined to the communal services and having felt powerless to affect their roles in reproductive and productive spheres, the children and grandchildren of the pioneer women sought some meaning and status in their lives. The socialist organisation of the mode of work excluded the bulk of women from productive high status labour activity and the egalitarian, bilineal organisation of kinship which operated at the level of a collective lineage has taken childrearing and domestic tasks away from the family and transformed them into the sphere of second class production. The traditional roles of women within feudal, peasant related or capitalist organisations of work and within the Jewish cultural organisation of ethnicity provided a statusful place for women within the context of the family. Women controlled the household and the rearing of the children which gave their lives a purpose, identity, and a chance, although a prescribed one, for self-fulfilment. Therefore, it is not contrary to such evidence that women who have been engaged in communal service activities which are defined as low status would seek to regain such status through traditional family roles that would give their lives meaning in the same manner that it did for their mothers, grandmothers and great-grandmothers or for women in Israeli society as a whole. In the wider Israeli society, the patriarchal family arrangement accords women a meaningful status of wife and mother and as Spiro notes a variety of tasks to perform (but within the wife-mother context), which could be viewed as a more attractive existence than that of collectivised, second class domestic labourers. These internal modes based on the Jewish organisation of ethnicity at the level of ethnic group coupled with the egalitarian organisation of kinship at the level of the collective lineage and the socialist organisation of work at the level of the community combined to produce a sex-role based occupational polarisation and the marginalisation of the majority of women from the productive processes and administration. This phenomenon which has occurred from the bottom up deriving from factors of culture, community and historical family based sex roles is serving to move the Kibbutz movement away from the social ideology of collectivism to that of individualism which is reflected in the demands of women towards greater familism. External factors deriving from the top down from the world economic order and nation state within the organisation of work are also affecting the moves towards familism among women and greater general individualism reinforcing the shift in social ideology from the pioneer days.

The linkages between the world economic order, the nation state and the collective

Israel from its inception has experienced a continuing struggle between priorities for national and class union. National unity has tended to prevail (Rayman 1981) and the Kibbutz movement has shared and been a part of the national entity. Necessarily, because of the Jewish organisation of ethnicity which the Kibbutzim share in common with Israel in terms of geography, language, religion, culture and heritage, the settlements have been an integral part of the social, political and economic life of Israel. The Kibbutz movement is therefore linked firmly to the state of Israel and comprises a sub-sector of a larger society which cannot insulate itself from those influences even if they are contrary to the socialistic and egalitarian social ideology of the Kibbutz movement (Rosner and Palgi 1980:14; Gerson 1978:13). By analogy Israel is also necessarily linked to the world economic order because of its small size and social, political and economic dependencies on Western nations such as America.

Israel, to which the Kibbutzim became an official constituent part, was not an advanced industrialised nation at the beginning of its statehood in 1948. It was relatively undeveloped and suffering withdrawal symptons from departing British colonialism such as an underdeveloped economy, a lack of infrastructure and territorial disputes with the internal and external Arab populations. It was therefore necessary for the Israeli nation to rely on capital imports from Western nations for industrialisation and development purposes. Capital imports to the state of Israel in the first twenty years consisted largely of donations, reparations from West Germany for Nazi atrocities, loans and grants from the United States government. The capital imports from the United States were to the Israeli government and did not affect the constitution of the Kibbutzim directly. Restitution money from West Germany in the minority of Kibbutzim was privately allocated with the majority distributing the monies collectively, so the effect during this period in the fifties was also relatively negligible to the organisation of the Kibbutzim (Rosner 1986; Gerson 1978:84). Israel received between the years 1948-68 more than seven and one half billion dollars of imports and goods than it had exported with only 30 per cent of the imported capital goods and services requiring a return outflow of interest, dividends or capital (Hanegbi 1971:5). Such capital inflows from Western nations facilitated the development of Israel technologically and industrially to a point where it could be ranked with advanced industrialised nations both economically and socially. These links with the world economic order were strengthened after the 1967 war and the incorporation of the West Bank, Sinai and the Gaza Strip. Foreign multinational companies were encouraged to join and invest in industrial as well as agricultural projects and investment conditions (i.e. tax codes) were liberalised. During the period between 1968-69, private companies were allowed to buy public enterprises and a compulsory wage freeze was instituted. Military expenditure increased to higher levels and in 1970 it comprised 24 per cent of the Gross National Product (Hanegbi 1971:7). Generally, the increased economic role of foreign capital coupled with greater military expenditure and economic input from the Territories acquired after 1967, resulted in changes in the Israeli political economy that paralleled the American technical level of industrialised standards of production.

The Kibbutzim have been most directly affected as an integral part of the Israeli nation in relation to their adoption of Western modes of technology and aspects of capitalist forms of the organisation of work. In the early days of the collectives mixed farming had predominated, while in later years, with increased industrialisation, agricultural specialisation became the primary form of farming. Accompanying the growth in mechanical farming was the requirement for specialists and technocrats from outside the collectives, who were used for advice and planning. The shift of capital investment from agricultural to industrial production which occurred in the post 1967 war years stimulated specialised, mainly light industrial production on many Kibbutzim. Such increases in specialisation and technological advancement, accompanied large rises in production. The specialisation of labour which is a feature central to capitalist industrialising societies, intensified during this period. In earlier days, the collectives were self-sufficient producers of agricultural commodities, while in more recent times they specialised in sink-unit production or flowers for export. To coordinate such economic activities, the Kibbutz system was required to depend on national marketing and production boards which linked Kibbutz production to the Israeli economy supporting the linkages between the collective settlements and the State. This specialisation of labour also reinforced the place of women within the collective service sectors as productive sectors were already established as a largely male domain and now required more specialised skills.

Accompanying the introduction of industrial plants during World War Two which were relatively large was the feature of hired labour on the Kibbutzim. In the sixties with the emphasis on small to medium size plants, the number of hired labourers was reduced, but features of the capitalist organisation of work that involves the hiring of labour remained. Hired labourers created incongruencies in the management system. Kibbutz members participation in decision making was affected because those members in production rather than management were subject to the hierarchical structure and supervision as were the hired workers (Rosner 1986:11-12).

With the introduction of new technology in the eighties the Kibbutz system is becoming every increasingly tied to market forces. All 260 of the collectives have an industrial plant and the most current figures for the eighties show that 53 per cent of the Kibbutz workforce are employed in production work in the industrial sectors. Kibbutz plants are also becoming increasingly competitors rather than complementary allies because of the limited size of the internal market in Israel and because the bulk of Kibbutzim have specialised in two major industrial branches of metals and plastics (Rosner 1987:10).

An accompanying feature of the new technology that presents a risk to the collective ethos is that of alienation in work roles and content. Agricultural work has traditionally proved to be more satisfying and less alienating for Kibbutz members offering greater diversity in terms of work opportunities. Industrial work continues to be perceived by Kibbutz members as less satisfying than agricultural labour, especially because it divides work along capitalist lines, dividing professional and production workers and offering limited opportunities for the latter. This dissatisfaction has occurred despite the efforts of the Kibbutz movement to avoid alienating forms of industrial technology such as the assembly line. Kibbutz members have also been interviewed about their feelings concerning the new technology before it is introduced and an effort has been made to make it user friendly. Production and everyday life on the Kibbutz are inextricably linked and are not alienated so that job satisfaction is essential for overall satisfaction with Kibbutz life. Pioneer ethics which viewed work solely in terms of a moral obligation has changed with the younger generation viewing work as both for the purposes of self-realisation and as a moral obligation (Rosner 1986:5-6; Rosner 1987). Work, therefore, both morally and for purposes of self-esteem, continues to be central to the life of Kibbutz members and the introduction of features of the capitalist organisation of work that fosters individualism, such as the hiring of labour, labour specialisation, inter-Kibbutz competition, thelack of job opportunities for production workers, may all contribute to the general move away from collectivity and the restoration of familism.

Women who work in the industrial plants experience a similar form of job dissatisfaction as do their male counterparts, but the majority of women have even less work opportunities and choice because they remain in the service sectors. Women have been allowed recently some choice in relation to the nature of their work in the service sectors with the introduction of the option to pursue further professional training and degrees. As material rewards and merit and social prestige are not necessarily linked, women experience the greatest equality in terms of the distribution of collective income, but fare less well in relation to status and merit (Shur and Peres 1986). The organisation of work on the Kibbutz continues to remain predominantly socialistic and women experience a high degree of economic income equality when compared to women in other nations in the world. Women, however, do experience a lack of job opportunities, social status and merit in their work which affects directly their feelings of self-worth and self-realisation. There are other extra-economic linkages between the collectives and the nation state that are affecting women's dissatisfaction with their role in the Kibbutz and their striving for self-worth and self-esteem through an increased familial role.

Extra-economic linkages between the collectives and the nation state that affect women

A national requirement that impinges upon the collectives and the social attitudes of women is the military service. All Israeli youth are required to serve in the military for a particular period in their late teens (excepting certain religious cases) and this obligation continues in later life in the form of the military service reserve. Women made a significant contribution to the defense of Jewish settlements and land prior to and at the inception of the State of Israel. After the growth of incipient nationalism under David Ben Gurion in the 1950's women were encouraged to contribute to Israeli society through an increase in their birthrate. This emphasis on the importance of women's reproductive activities has permeated the army and is strongly in evidence today. Women are viewed as restraining influences on males who wish to exhibit unruly behaviour. They are also viewed as having their own sphere separate from that of men, which is an ideology reflected on the army radio station that broadcasts programmes for female soldiers dealing with cosmetic application and beauty. The Israel Defense Forces (I.D.F.) summarisation of the role of Women's Corps (Chen) stresses family-related service activities (Hecht and Davis 1979: 93).[2]

The Israeli media, similar to the military emphasises the importance of women's family and domestic duties, and it glorifies the role of housewife. Women in the cities are presented as living a rewarding and private existence through studying at universities, raising their own children and generally experiencing a more varied life than the Kibbutz system is believed to offer it's members. Many women on the collectives feel that women living within the privatised family lead a more desirable way of life because they may utilise their educational skills more fully and pursue occupations of their own choosing. The idea that women outside the Kibbutz movement experience a fuller, more rewarding life has caused women to encourage their families to move to the towns and cities and to cooperative Moshavim. The Moshavim however, do not appear to provide the most satisfactory circumstances for women because although the household chores which women perform are recognised as productive work worthy of remuneration, 90 per cent of women and 85 per cent of men interviewed on a number of Moshavim supported the idea of occupational training for their daughters. Moshav members were fearful that their daughters would be frustrated and leave the Moshavim if they could not obtain fulfilling occupations (Gerson 1978:55).

Another factor that affects women which occurs within the organisation of ethnicity at the level of tribe is the inter-tribal conflict between the Ashkenazi Jews who originated from Hebrew tribes and settled in nations of the West and Eastern Europe and the Sephardic (Oriental) Jews who derived from Hebrew tribes and settled in Arab, Persian, Indian and Southern European nations. Both groups derived originally from the twelve tribes of Israel who were resident in the région known historically as Judea and Israel and were dispersed from this ancient homeland by the Romans who had called the land Palestina, (after the Philistines).

The Kibbutz system which was founded and settled largely by Ashkenazi Jews has been experiencing an influx of Oriental Jews since the 1950's. The Oriental Jewish members of the Kibbutz movement, who bring with them traditional social organisation have a kinship structure that is patrilineal and patriarchal with wife and mother the primary roles for women. Oriental Jewish mothers care for their children differently in such activities as nursing and weaning, which often conflicts with Kibbutz practice. Oriental parents, for example, may attempt to protect their girl children and encourage their boys to be aggressive, which would be in direct conflict with the cooperative ethos of equal opportunity that constitutes the foundation of the social ideology of the Kibbutzim (Gerson 1978:115). Therefore, women from the Sephardic background may be inclined towards greater familism because of their cultural heritage.

A related factor concerns women who in-marry into the Kibbutz. Many studies have shown that in-marrying women who were not born on a Kibbutz nor educated there, were the least committed to Kibbutz values and were the most enthusiastic supporters of greater moves towards individual familism. Non-Kibbutz born women tended to support strongly demands for increased family authority and children sleeping with their families (Rosner and Palgi 1980:14).

The influx of Oriental Jews and in-marrying non-Kibbutz members, represent a weakening of the collective, socialist social ideology because the process of self-selection of those most committed to egalitarian ideals is no longer as strong as in the pioneering days and is not the primary motive for some non-Kibbutz members to live in the collective settlements (Shur and Peres 1986:336). Additionally, generations subsequent to those of the pioneers have not chosen to be born into the Kibbutz system, nor do they have a history of reacting violently against persecution in a foreign country. Subsequently, the Sabra generations lack the self-selected fervour of the original settlers who as a part of their great commitment to the underlying egalitarian social ideology were also reacting intensely against the capitalism and persecution of their native societies in Eastern and Western Europe.

The recent shift, which has varied according to the Kibbutz group in question, from collective social ideological emphasis to individual whatever the degree, is reflected in the combined changes within the combination modes of the organisation of work, kinship and ethnicity. The organisation of ethnicity acts as a unifying force between the Kibbutz system and the State of Israel making the former a sub-sector of Israeli society in general. The organisation of work through the levels of the world economic order and nation state have incorporated the Kibbutzim into Western modes of technology that are capitalist in orientation and market forces. At the level of the community and related to the organisation of kinship, a sexual division of labour which has persisted from the inception of the Kibbutz system, has placed the majority of women at the level of the lineage, in the collective services sector performing largely repetitive, tedious tasks without the status or variety that the nuclear or extended family offers. Therefore, given the general movement of the Kibbutz system from collectivity to individualism and the dissatisfaction of women with their occupational roles the move towards familism represents an underlying internal social ideological shift, but certainly not the demise of the Kibbutz movement.[3]

We have seen in the case of the Kibbutz which is a socialist micro-society within a larger capitalist one how the combination modes theory explains the process of social change specific to this system. The organisation of ethnicity is a prominent mode in this social equation as the desire of the Jewish people to return to their ancient homeland provided the social ideological impetus to establish the first Kibbutzim. The next and final case study that utilises the combination modes theory as a mode of analysis is that of China, which social ideologically transformed from a feudal nation to one that subscribed to state socialism. We will be assessing the reasons why the commune system was not substained along with a more equal role in society for women, which has led to the present system.

Notes

1. As sex equality is more efficient at the micro-level of the family, women are more drawn to the family because of greater sex equality at that level. Women are able to exert increased direct pressure on men at the emotional micro-level of the family in direct proportion to men's increased involvement.

2. The role of the Women's Corp (Chen) is summarised by the I.D.F. in the following manner (Hecht and Davies 1979:93).

   (1) Indirect reinforcement of the I.D.F's combat forces, by fulfilling a variety of administration, professional and service duties, thus releasing a larger number of soldiers for fighting missions.

   (2) Preparing women to defend themselves, their families and homes, due to the unique security circumstances of Israel.

   (3) Assisting in the I.D.F's education and social enterprise... and participating in the national extra-military missions of the I.D.F. as an absorbent of immigration, tutor and rehabilitation of social disadvantaged youth, etc.

3. Comments and criticisms by Professor Menachem Rosner in both correspondence and discussion in relation to women, family and the Kibbutz system have been most valuable for the construction of this chapter. (He is the founder and director of the Institute for Research of the Kibbutz and the Cooperative Idea University of Haifa and founder member of Kibbutz Reshefim).

3 The Chinese commune: state socialist development

This chapter concentrates on the commune period of recent Chinese history, because it was one of the most tumultuous times of social change and was a radical departure from the prevailing social ideology of Chinese feudalism. This historical period also presented an unprecedented opportunity for Chinese women to break from the strict control of the patriarchal order and assert themselves as valued, equal members of society who have been fully incorporated into production. Although gains for women occurred during the height of the commune system, such changes diminished with the dissolution of the communes and the institution of the present system. Utilising the combination modes thesis, it is proposed that patrilineal kinship organisation was not challenged fully by the Chinese Communist Party (CCP), which maintained the lineage/family/household as a economic unit of production impeding the transformation to an egalitarian mode of kinship. The failure of the patriarchal mode of kinship to transform to an egalitarian one initiated change towards the capitalist mode of the organisation of work from the bottom up at the levels of the lineage/family/household. This has caused in varying degrees, labour becoming organised along capitalist lines, greater inequities in the distribution of wealth and resources and the re-incorporation of China into the world economic order. It has also contributed to the dissolution of the commune system, the tendency towards pre-revolutionary private ownership of land, and limitations in the establishment of equal rights for women.

The initial dissolution of the feudal order occurred through the penetration of Western nations into China and its subsequent division into foreign dominated spheres of influence. The CCP arose as a reaction against the degrading effects of foreign influence and subsequent internal decay, which gave rise to the commune system and extricated China from the world economic order. Therefore, we shall assess the historical linkages at different levels of the combination modes which allowed social movement down from the world economic order to the levels of the lineages/families/households and then up towards the world economic order.

The organisation of ethnicity in terms of inter-ethnic group conflict within China, such as among the Han Chinese and the Hakkas or external groupings such as the Uigurs, Tibetans or Vietnamese is marginal in terms of impact on the commune system and changes in the position of women. The organisation of ethnicity is most relevant in relation to the cultural peculiarities of the predominant Chinese Han national groupings.

Theoretical implications

In relation to Chinese socialism which was instituted during the inception of the commune system, the bulk of researchers who have studied the changing position of women in China argue that while the CCP has ameliorated the worst excesses against women found in feudal times, women are not liberated to any great degree from traditional oppression (Wolf 1985; Andors 1983, 1981, 1976; Stacy 1983, 1979; Weinbaum 1982, 1978. 1976; Wang 1980; Croll 1980; Murray 1979; Diamond 1975; Salaff and Merkle 1973).

The commune system represented a marked change in social organisation for the bulk of the Chinese populace. The vast majority of the populace resided in the countryside and continue to do so with 80 per cent living currently in rural areas (Andors 1983:79). Throughout the duration of the commune system and especially at its inception, the position of women changed the most rapidly. While it is generally agreed among scholars who have assessed the Chinese commune system that many positive gains have been made for women, their findings show that the emancipation of women has been achieved only partially on the rural collectives (Wolf 1985; Stacy 1983; Croll 1980; Thorborg 1978; Davin 1976; Diamond 1975). The reasons for the weakened relationship between Chinese socialism in the form of the communes and the emancipation of women centres on the relation of women to the lineage/family/household levels of society. In relation to arguments of the world system theorists who suggest that socialist countries such as China are weakened largely and changed by external mechanisms of unequal exchange and production relations with advanced 'core' countries, I would argue that in the case of China internal socioeconomic structures have also initiated social change. The organisation of kinship based on patrilineal inheritance which the CCP only challenged superficially at the level of the lineage has provided obstacles to the attempted transformation to the socialist mode of the organisation of work and the liberation of women from the subordinate roles allotted to women in traditional society.

China's incorporation into the world economic order

The penetration of China by Western nations began in the seventeenth and eighteenth centuries because Imperial China of the Ming and Ch'ing dynasties was viewed by the West as rich in natural resources and goods (Moulder 1977:98). The Chinese were largely successful in forestalling Western encroachment until a marked change in trading relations occurred in the nineteenth century. Britain, the most powerful imperial seafaring nation at this historical period accelerated its actions in opening up China as a market for the burgeoning Western textile industry to redress the tea trade imbalance. Britain's success in drawing the Chinese political economy into the world market was produced through the introduction of Indian grown opium. The consumption of opium expanded in China dramatically with the result that '... by the mid 1820's the outflow of silver from China actually exceeded the inflow, probably for the first time in modern history' (Moulder 1977:102). The Chinese people because of the introduction of opium suffered the social consequences of addiction and increased pauperisation.

Britain's attempts to create a market for their textiles proved to be so successful that by the latter half of the 1920's, 60 per cent of annually consumed clothing was purchased on the market in Northern China, while 98 per cent of yearly consumed clothing was bought in Southern and Eastern China. By the late 1920's, especially in the heavily foreign penetrated south eastern coastal parts, textiles manufacture in foreign owned factories worked by cheap Chinese labour had doubled from the early 1900's (Weinbaum 1976:35-6). The opening of the Chinese markets by Britain also allowed other industrial powers such as the U.S.A. France and Germany to encroach upon the Chinese markets.

China's economic incorporation into the world economic order was firmly entrenched by the 1920's, with a political incorporation parallel to the economic one. Complex and inter-related Western economic investments in shipbuilding and repairs, internal and external transport such as railways, manufacturing, banking, mines and loans with high interest rates charged to the Chinese government in the late nineteenth, early twentieth centuries was accompanied by political incorporation. Two major wars, the Opium War (1840-1842) and the Second Opium War (1858-1860) resulted in the defeat of the Chinese by the British, with the increased weakening of the former through indemnity payments and treaties that caused the further erosion of the Chinese political economy (Purcell 1980).

China's budding capitalism and its emergent incorporation into the world economic order in the early twentieth century affected Chinese social organisation, leading eventually to the formation of the commune system and influencing the position of women. The impact of China's incorporation into the world economic order and the rise of the capitalist organisation of work on women at this historical juncture of social change may be assessed through the example of the Chinese silk industry.

The position of women changes within the foreign dominated silk industry

Capitalist penetration into the indigenous silk industry began in the 1870's and it caused a dislocation in the peasant based household operation. Silk that was produced for export had to meet the requirements of the buyers. The West being the major consumers of silk imposed a high standard on raw silk production, which had the effect of displacing female home producers who practiced the unsuitable hand-reeling method that did not meet Western requirements.

Home silk spinning declined rapidly because female reelers could not compete with the quality and high production levels of factory produced silk thread. By the late nineteenth, early twentieth century, home produced silk thread was replaced by factory manufactured thread. With the rising international demand for silk and higher world market prices, greater rural industrialisation occurred coupled with socioeconomic reorganisation at the levels of the community and household. The demand for labour increased along with the rise in modern silk-reeling factories and silk weaving handicraft workshops. As the capitalist organisation of work articulated with the feudal organisation of work, the emerging capital based economy predominated, which made wages essential to the survival of the peasant household.

Silk production was reorganised into handicraft workshops and men replaced women as silk weavers earning relatively high wages. Young males were organised under master-weavers and assisted in agricultural production during the busy season (Sun 1922). Women, as peasant wives were displaced from the productive sector or were relegated to low paid handspinning subsidiary silk work, while as daughters they were used to supply modern silk-reeling factories with compliant, largely unskilled diligent workers. Females although unskilled in manufacturing work were trained in the delicate procedures of silk-making because of their gender socialisation in domestic tasks within the family.

Young, unmarried daughters became a new, wage earning class for a number of reasons that relate to the reorganisation of the mode of work and kinship at this particular historical period. Capitalist industry recruited girls for the factories because as in present day Malaysia young, unmarried females were believed to be proficient in the manipulation of materials, compliant in accordance with the passive role inculcated in the family and cheap, healthy labour. Such factories often stipulated that they did not want married women, mothers or elderly females as workers.

Daughters as in the Malaysian case study, were the most dispensable members of the household as they would be lost eventually in marriage. Fathers were needed to work the land, despite meagre returns, while sons were required to attract brides who could add to family fortune, gain inheritance and continue the family line. Mothers, on the other hand, were necessary for the reproduction of children, domestic production for exchange, and the organisation of household tasks (Fei 1980:47, 233-35; Weinbaum 1976:38). All family members were required to participate in production to meet the survival needs of the household. Families attempted willingly for survival purposes to send at least one daughter to work in the factories in the towns.

Silk work as performed by females was one of the 'higher' paid occupations in the early twentieth century. It paid approximately two hundred dollars per annum for two hundred and fifty working days. This sum was the income on which a family of five could minimally survive in addition to subsistence production (So and Cheng 1981:7). Daughters experienced a degree of independence unknown in traditional society by having wages paid directly to them; although they were obliged to give some if not all of their wages to the heads of the household (Chia) because family organisation remained basically intact. Girls were allowed to spend some of their earnings on clothing or other necessities and mother often retained a portion of the wages for the future dowry of their daughters. It was not unusual for young brides to be encouraged to continue their factory work, to supplement their husbands' family income. Mothers-in-law in these circumstances had their control over their daughters-in-law substantially weakened and were compelled to assist the latter in such household chores as meal preparation (Fei 1980: 234-35). Daughters-in-law who worked for wages were considered a good marriage investment.

Despite the relatively high wages of female silk workers, the bulk of profit accrued to the factory owners and working conditions were poor. Female silk workers were usually crowded into dark, poorly ventilated rooms without rest areas in over 90 degree (Farenheit) heat, working an average of 11½ hours per day with a half hour lunch break, seven days a week.

The workers were required to perform very delicate tedious tasks under severe pressure, as mistakes in the silk reeling procedure were deducted from their wages. Women over 30 years of age, were usually suspended from work because they often became unemployable through ailing eyesight and general deterioration in their health. Supervisors were usually males who often abused female workers both mentally and physically. They also controlled important decision making regarding employment and the type or amount of fines levied for unsatisfactory work (So and Cheng 1981:8-9; Chen 1922:143).

Familial hierarchy was reinforced rather than weakened in the factories because the male supervision of females reflected the sexual divisions that were found within the family at all levels. Tensions between male and female workers increased as male silk weavers operating machine-powered looms lost their jobs to female silk workers in the factories. Men often opposed the female silk workers violently. The prestige of male family members was challenged by unmarried daughters or young brides who had gained primary earning status because of the decline in returns from agricultural labour and silk weaving workshops. The loss of status occurred despite the rights of the eldest male of the household to the wages of the female members (Weinbaum 1976:40).

Resistance to marriage or the consumation of marriage by significant numbers of female silk workers occurred predominantly in the area of the Canton delta. Sankar (1978) and others believe that marriage resistance represented a weakening in lineage solidarity. Lineage solidarity Sankar (1978) suggests was weakened because of the rise of the capitalist factory system, which was accompanied by increasing class stratification within lineages.[1] In my estimation, lineage solidarity and retention of wealth was strengthened not weakened and class stratification helped to consolidate lineage organisation. In the cases of wealthier lineage members exploiting poorer members as cheap labour for silk factories, the former were able to exert greater pressure on the latter to prevent strikes for example, because poorer members were family. Family pressure and rules of obedience were implemented most effectively among other related lineage members. Where entire lineages constituted one class stratum, solidarity was increased because the lineage in it's traditional manner reshaped itself according to the newly emerging capitalist economic order to even further consolidate family wealth. Such consolidation of wealth was the raison d'etre of the patrilineally based lineages.

Lower class lineages/families/households, following the example of upper class lineages, had previously scorned women working outside the home, castigating unmarried working females as harlots. When upper class lineages invested in silk production because agriculture was in decline, causing lower class lineages/families/households to depend on their unmarried daughters' wages and the upper classes to depend on the cheap labour of lower class females, social attitudes to non-marriage and females working outside the home altered. Girls' houses were instituted for example, and were seen to protect female modesty. Non-marriage celibacy, which was economically necessary for many female silk workers who were required to work long hours and support their natal families, acquired religious overtones of a nun-like nature. Spinster vegetarian halls, homes and temples were built with particular ceremonies being created to lend this new institution social sanction (Sankar 1978:118; Topley 1978:68). Lineages/families/households therefore reshaped themselves according to the new economic requirements. They viewed their female kin as workers, taking pride in the fact that their clan members were accumulating wealth for the lineage, not for the individual female. Lineages consequently viewed strikes by their female members as a threat to their vested interests and the lineages supported the capitalist factory owners, who were sometimes members of their own ranks, in the event of strikes occurring. Lineage authorities were so hostile to strikes, that if the police and army working for capitalist/landlord lineage factory owners were not able to break a strike. lower class families expelled their members unless the recalcitrant female labourers returned to work. They often drowned strike leaders in pig cages (Fairbank 1967:36-37). Strikes by female workers served to disrupt their important economic contribution to the family and had the potential to challenge lineage authority because females were not performing passively their socioeconomic function which might have led to a general rebellion by females and a subsequent undermining of family hierarchy.

External and internal pressures leading to the rise of the commune system

Tensions existed therefore at the levels of the lineage/family/household within the organisation of kinship that threatened to change the nature of the Chinese family and the position of women. The Chinese family adapted to aspects of change that allowed it to continue to survive but resisted rebellion by women workers which threatened to disrupt the family further.

Intense change at the level of the world economic order within the organisation of work occurred at this historical juncture, affecting the economic stability of China at the level of the nation state and the community. To continue with the example of the silk industry, by the late 1920's and early 1930's, the silk market began to collapse because of the world economic slump. The depressed state of agriculture deepened with the increased penetration of the capitalist market system that required peasant tenants to pay rent in cash from rice sales. The level of rice production remained the same, but rice prices were driven down on the market because peasants had to sell their rice to pay the rent, which caused them to sell greater amounts of rice and to eat into their reserves. Peasants were often forced to buy high priced rice on the market for survival. Loans had to be obtained for survival purposes and usurious landlords charged high interest rates (Fei 1980:185:86). The collapse of industrial life in 1935, caused the majority of silk factories to close. Daughters who had been providing the main source of income for their families, lost their jobs which caused mass starvation. Many female silk workers were not able to return to their villages, because their families, already near starvation did not allow them to return to their homes. Many lower class peasants from the Southern provinces attempted to emigrate, but males because of the worldwide depression, were no longer allowed into Southeast Asian countries. Initially, there were few quotas on female emigration to Southeast Asian countries. Families urged their daughters to emigrate so that they could obtain work as domestic servants sending money back to the family/lineage (Topley 1978:84-85).

For an economy so reliant on the world economic order, the depression of world silk market prices was a disaster for silk producing areas, causing severe social disruption and plunging the silk producing Chinese countryside into chaos. The external factors of worldwide depression, foreign imperialism coupled with the internal factors of the rise of the warlords in the countryside, the fall of the last imperial dynasty, the increasing replacement of feudalism by capitalism and tensions within the family all aided in facilitating social change in China, giving rise to the CCP, the extrication of China from the world economic order and the establishment of the commune system.

The Chinese family whether it constituted the idealised lineage form which was more prevalent in the wealthier South, South-east regions or the extended family of the poorer Northern regions, has been an enduring and tenacious feature of Chinese history. To understand the position of women in Chinese society and how they and the commune were affected by the social, economic and political turmoil that led to the inception of the commune system it is essential to assess women's traditional role within the organisation of kinship and how the family provided an island of stability within a sea of change.

The traditional lineage/family/household

The organisation of kinship at the levels of the lineage/family/household was central historically to Chinese social structure. These kinship forms, based on patrilineal residence linked social relations to the organisation of work at the level of the community. Inheritance of both title and property was patrilineal. While age and sex stratification existed within the lineage family, the focus of the individual centered on the collectivity. Collective resources were utilised to diversify financial interests, strengthen the collective clan and to control weaker and lower class lineage families. Landlord lineages expanded their financial investments into the most profitable individual and rural sectors, consolidating their interests as rural landlords, state officials and burgeoning capitalists.

All female clan members were subject to exogamous marriage and lived with the family of the husband. Women had a strictly defined subordinate place within the clans of their husbands, but after becoming established through bearing sons and grandsons, often became powerful members of their husbands' lineages. Female peasants of the lower classes were oppressed by both men and women of the wealthy lineages as servants, slaves and tenants or as female workers.

The Chinese Communist Party stripped the wealthy single surname lineages of their landlord/official/rich peasant leadership and their religious functions, but left the actual patrilineally based kinship structure intact (Diamond 1975:27). A number of theorists argue that the CCP left the patrilineal kinship organisation intact purposefully, while others suggest that they did so inadvertently. Wolf (1985:16-18) and Johnson (1983) argue that the CCP emphasised production drives and that the 1934 Marriage Law, women's associations and other reforms to emancipate women were de-emphasised in reality. Land reform Wolf suggests was used to undermine the importance of the Marriage Law of May 1950 as women were used mainly in the struggle against the landlord stratum. The fact that women were given land was rendered valueless because men continued to own women as property and could transfer both them and their property to other families. Stacy (1983) believes that the CCP never intended to disturb the patriarchal basis of Chinese society, but actually promised the population a stable family life within the traditional patriarchal context. Whether it was intentional or inadvertent in intent and although former lineage leaders were stigmatised and divested of their wealth, the lineages as a whole were not viewed as class enemies. Patrilocal residence which kept women in a subordinate position to patrilineal clansmen was maintained and not challenged.

Lineages/families/households remain economic units of production on the communes

The organisation of kinship of the traditional patrilineal Chinese family at the levels of the lineage/family/household was strengthened rather than weakened after the establishment of the communes which had an adverse effect on the position of women. This patrilineal organisation of kinship was combined in terms of the combination modes theory with an organisation of ethnicity and work particular to the Chinese case. Ancestor worship combined with a common language, custom and ritual, which had both a kinship and religious ethnic function, made the family unit a strong central part of traditional Chinese life. These kinship and ethnic forms, particularly characteristic to China, retained their strong links to the social relations of work because the communal collectives were based on the same natural system of villages, lineages and neighbourhoods found in traditional society. Patrilineally based village structure coupled with the strengthening of the organisation of kinship at the levels of the extended family and lineage to the social relations of work, continued to maintain women as subordinates to male kin lineages, households and extended families in a number of ways.

The process of communisation divided collectives into the natural village pattern, which housed lineages and gave new focus to lineage loyalty. Teams and brigades for example, often held the same male kinship base, with some smaller production teams being referred to by lineage surname and clansmen dominating all local leadership positions. This occurred as well in multi-surname villages, in which former wealthy lineages used their past prestige and numbers to assume local hegemony. Wealthy lineages were deprived of their scattered landholdings after land reform, but especially in the case of single surname lineages, the clans retained their local rich village lands. The retention of local land allowed the single surname teams/brigades who comprised the wealthy, single surname lineage landlord, rich peasant classes before 1949 to become the most prosperous teams. The single surname lineage teams were the most efficient and believed themselves to be superior to former lower class lineages. Teams that belonged to the poorest, weakest lineages in the pre-1949 period became the poorest most disorganised communes in the following three decades. The poorer peasants were not able to move into wealthy lineage villages because of high rents, clan solidarity and physical intimidation. After 1950, peasant mobility was equally restricted because of severe governmental migration restraints. Government policy did not allow migration to other communes or to urban areas which permitted inadvertently the wealthy lineage based teams to increase their wealth and the less prosperous teams to remain weak and poor (Parish and Whyte 1978:58-9). Male mobility was not approved by the government because if allowed, the poor communes would have been depleted of much needed male labour, while the prosperous collectives would have become overburdened with able-bodied male labourers (Parish 1975:616-25;

Byung-joon 1975:650-51). Kinship organisation at the level of the lineages was supported by governmental policy indirectly because it maintained patrilocal residence and exogamous marriage. The extended patrilineal form of kinship organisation was naturally maintained because the family remained the major socioeconomic support in the countryside and individuals needed to have many relatives and build political alliances to survive (Wolf 1985:144).

The necessity for family based survival supported patrilineal based lineage organisation as an economic unit. The welfare system in traditional Chinese society, relied on male children caring for aged parents. The only insurance parents had concerning infirmities of old age was their sons. Therefore, most parents wanted at least two sons, in the eventuality that one son became ill or indisposed. Sons were encouraged by the government to care for their parents regardless of the wealth or poverty of the production team. A family that had only daughters was in a very weak position in relation to welfare for the elderly. Some parents in this situation arranged matrilocal marriages, whereby the sons-in-law provided support for them in their old age. Matrilocal marriage was not popular because it placed men in a subordinate position. Single surname lineage based teams or brigades in particular resented sharing grain and authority functions with outsider males. Government restrictions on male mobility for reasons noted above, had the unintended effect of strengthening the traditional reliance on sons to care for aging parents, thus further strengthening the patrilineal family lineage.

Inter-communal/brigade/team income inequality based on the family as an economic unit of production was strengthened indirectly by the integration of females into the productive process. This government policy had intended to facilitate the socialist mode of organisation of work and the liberation of women from traditional roles as unremunerated family labourers. As women became income earning labourers, the dowry was replaced by a full bride price system in the countryside, contributing to inter-team inequality. Families believed that because daughters added to family income through agricultural labour, they were entitled to adequate compensation for the loss of earnings upon marriage. Families were prepared to pay a high bride price, because they would be compensated by their daughters-in-law extra income and household labour. The value of daughters also increased because their earnings were used to pay for their brothers' brides. Because families wanted their daughters to marry the most prosperous lineage/families, wealthy villagers paid the lowest bride prices, while less wealthy villagers were required to offer high bride prices with the result that many families became debtors. This was especially the case with less wealthy lineage/family/households who were also recipients of the least desirable brides.

Although women accepting a bride price were given certain rights and claims to property as long as they remained a part of their husband's family, they lost their rights upon divorce. In the case of divorce, cadres often supported the claims of the parents-in-law for repayment of the bride price, despite the fact that such monetary exchanges were illegal. Some families avoided the bride price system by exchanging daughters among themselves (Parish and Whyte 1978:185-87, 190-3, 196). Yet, the majority of families in the countryside did participate in some form of bride price system with the poorer teams paying the highest prices while often obtaining the least hardworking, lowest point earning brides.

Exogamous marriage continued to be normative. A practice underpinning exogamy was that of wu-fu which traditionally banned marriages between members of the same surname, despite its discouragement in the modern government marriage law. Exogamy continued to be practiced by all Chinese families from the smallest (the simple) to the largest (the lineage) (Baker 1979:1-3). In-marrying brides remained at a disadvantage in both their natal and adopted villages, despite their newly acquired point earning capability. As daughters, they continued to be viewed by their lineages/families/households as temporary residents who departed upon marriage and no longer contributed to their natal families' finances. Male children continued to be preferred because girls did not continue the family line. Girls were not usually recommended by the household team or brigade for specialised training, higher education or training for positions of leadership and responsibility because this was deemed a waste of much needed resources on a group of individuals who would shortly depart for another team or brigade. Young women, arriving at their new team and brigade were an unknown quantity who were required to prove themselves before they were recommended for training or higher education (Diamond 1975:27-8). Schools were village based, allowing males to receive continuous education and training. Patrilocal placement of schools supported lineage solidarity and the status of women as outsiders.

The major focus for social change in the CCP was private property and the landlord class that controlled lineage power. Wolf (1985:188) notes that the ideological base of landlord/lineage power was ignored because it was not viewed as a threat to the state and it was believed that any reorganisation of Chinese kinship relations could be left to the natural erosion of societal change. Despite the intentions of the state administration, kinship ties and family loyalties have prevailed, especially among the same surname production teams (Wolf 1985:151). Fenghuo Brigade in Shaanxi, for example, was comprised of the old lineage organisation with all women having married outside of their clan group. Lineage exogamy served to maintain harmonious relations among kin members and their daughters' families. The Brigade continued in its traditional pattern of life with such practices as arranged marriages (Wolf 1985:166). The CCP had greater success in establishing non-lineage families in the urban centres, which has and continues to constitute a minute proportion of the population. In the rural areas farm families continued to aspire to the multi-generational families and have used any prosperity brought by the commune system and in recent years to realise this ideal. The state never supported multi-generational families but the peasants strived for this ideal because in the past poverty destroyed families, while the advent of the commune system provided stability which facilitated family relationships.

The Chinese government administration was not anti-family, rather it attempted to weaken the power of the landlord stratum without destroying the social and economic functions of the domestic unit such as production, consumption and care of the elderly. Neither did all regions of China practice strong lineage organisation, although all Chinese families whether nuclear, stem, or grand, were patrilineally based, venerated their elders and believed women to be inferior to kin members (Wolf 1985:184-85, 188). Women also remained outsiders in the bulk of Chinese families, torn in allegiance between patrilineal kin and exogamous based kinship networks during occurences of inter-lineage, inter-family hostilities that remained from traditional days.

Women as structural links between the organisation of work and kinship in the commune system

Patrilineal kinship organisation at the levels of the lineage/family/household remained an economic unit of production, while the class structure of the organisation of work being linked to kinship organisation reinforced the socioeconomic functions of the kinship unit. The particular, subordinate position of women continued to remain essential to the maintenance of Chinese social organisation. This was because womens' roles as reproducers of male kin, producers, domestic labourers, maintainers of family wealth and socialisers of future generations provided the structural links necessary for the existence of the patriarchal based mode of the organisation of kinship and class based changing order of feudalism to capitalism within the organisation of work. The various social roles of women essential to the maintenance of linkages between kinship organisation of work so conditioned the socioeconomic order of Chinese society historically, that these roles changed little with the establishment of the commune system. The commune system as noted did not challenge to any great extent the organisation of the traditional Chinese family.

Childbearing practices did not alter substantially. Fathers continued to discipline the children and maintain a distanced, reserved relationship especially with sons, while mothers were viewed as sympathetic family members who did not take the responsibility for discipline. The government encouraged families to use verbal persuasion for discipline, but in practice corporal punishment remained the most widely used form of discipline. Children remained the property of their parents with other villagers reluctant to interfere in the disciplining of children lest it lead to village disharmony. Children continued to be raised traditionally, with the sexual division of labour taught from infancy and practiced from five or six years of age.

Rural families, especially female members, continued to raise their children to be family centered and obedient to their parents. Family centered socialisation was reinforced in the family by elders and in the nurseries by grandmothers, older girls or the women in charge. Nurseries, which existed mainly in the wealthier villages, were usually staffed by grandmothers or older girls who ensured that the children did not harm themselves, while their parents worked in the fields. Many women withdrew their children from the nurseries, not wishing to spend the extra money and/or because they were dissatisfied with the women in charge who sometimes gave preferential treatment to their own children while neglecting the other youngsters. Most Chinese children on the communes were kept at their homes, under the care of a grandmother or an older girl (Parish and Whyte 1978:233; Parish 1975:620). Grandmothers often socialised the children in traditional ways that encouraged kin loyalty, sex typing (Mydral 1966) and a general mode of behaviour that reinforced the patriarchal organisation of kinship.

The family continued to be considered a private sphere which reinforced ideas of lineage/family loyalty; the primary role of women as reproducers; and a rigid form of kinship organisation that reinforced the general social structure of Chinese society with hierarchies based on sex and age. Although cadres were exhorted by government policy to extend socialist political ideology based on class struggle to the local family level, the constraints of operating within a network of patrilineal kinsmen militated against such actions as punishment for wifebeaters. Cadres, remaining subject to family restraints, did not relish intervention in their private affairs (Parish and Whyte 1978:216). Croll (1978:20) notes that there were three obstacles to divorce, the husband, the mother-in-law and the cadres. The latter presented the greatest problem as their cooperation was more important on the local level than the laws of marriage reform. The Marriage Law of 1950 sought to destroy the economic power of the landlord lineages and personal problems such as divorce were viewed as secondary to the economy (Wolf 1985:1).

Patrilocal residence and exogamous marriage reinforced structurally the most traditional and frequent family conflict that occurred between daughters-in-law and mothers-in-law (Wolf 1985:230). This conflict arose because of the weak position of women as both disadvantaged in-marrying strangers and those who were essential for keeping family wealth intact. Mothers-in-law had greater influence in the family than young brides because they had gained power by producing male heirs for patrilineal clansmen. Women derived power from influencing male family members, and the conflict between mothers and daughters-in-law was particularly bitter because they were competing for power through control over the same men. The husband-wife relationship remained weak because sons continued to inherit parental property and women remained 'outsiders' within the family context (Baker 1979:191-92).

Consanguinity between parents and their sons continued to be strong because sons depended on their parents for housing (which unlike the bulk of village land, was privately owned), the brideprice payments and any household items necessary for a new home. The average commune income was usually not large enough to buy a house or to pay a brideprice. Poorer married couples lived with the husbands' parents, while sons from wealthier families built a new house attached to the house of their parents. Women contributed their income and domestic services for the collective financial gain of the household, but they did not receive inheritance to which they were legally entitled, child custody or property rights after divorce. Patrilineal residence therefore, which underpinned the strength of the lineages, required women as structural links between the patriarchal organisation of kinship and the budding socialist organisation of work, but in a weakened capacity. These circumstances left women in an inferior position which also maintained the family as an economic unit of production and consumption that inhibited socialism from being implemented at the local level. Chinese peasant women did join men in all aspects of agricultural production earning their own workpoints from the inception of the commune system (Thorborg 1978:536-96). However, women were responsible for domestic work and often received a lower number of work points and less interesting jobs. Domestic labour constituted a severe double burden for women as housework continued to be regarded as the responsibility of women who were expected to manage successfully with repetitive household chores in addition to agricultural labour and political activity. Governmental directives encouraged equal pay for equal work and shared housework (Diamond 1975:29), but the strength of patrilineally based family organisation prevented these measures from being implemented successfully. Resistance against governmental attempts to institute equal pay and some form of shared housework may be noted in the first goverment directive entitled, 'Decision on the Development of APC's of 1953', which stipulated equal pay for equal work to mobilise women for agricultural needs. The establishment of the first rural commune in the late 1950's was accompanied by a production drive, the Great Leap Forward, which emphasised self-sacrifice and the betterment of society rather than personal gain. Women were relieved of many household tasks through the establishment of collective canteens, nurseries, laundries and other services so that they were free to participate in production. Equal pay was not emphasised and many women subsequently did not make a maximum effort in their work because their pecuniary reward was so much lower than that of men, and because they remained responsible for certain household tasks despite communal services. Stacy (1982) argues that during the Great Leap Forward women were recruited to help the economy. Communal arrangements were made to facilitate the role of women in maintaining production drives. After the failure of the Great Leap Forward in 1960, resources were scarce and service organisations on the communes were closed, requiring women to perform household tasks on an individual basis. Services to aid women in household chores were sacrificed without resistance from women or men because the former had traditionally performed these tasks without remuneration or social assistance and their needs were not considered to be paramount. Additionally, communal services were disliked by the majority of peasants, who preferred their own family domestic arrangements (Mydral 1966). Strong resistance from patrilineally based kinship networks that opposed inter-family mixing which may have weakened patrilineal inheritance, furthered the demise of domestic services organised on a communal basis.

The government at this point attempted to attract women to field work with the promise of equal pay because men were needed for capital construction projects. Equal pay alone, which was never uniformly implemented throughout the countryside, did not substantially increase women's productive labour participation. The subsequent Cultural Revolution which attempted to regain political control for Mao Tse-Tung did involve women and actually attacked the traditional family. The Cultural Revolution was unsuccessful and had negligible long-term effects with many women believing that their new found voice within the home was the liberation that they had been seeking (Croll 1978:24-25).

Following the Cultural Revolution, a synthesis of earlier government policies was proposed, calling for equal pay for women and assistance with household chores in the form of husbands and grandmothers aiding with domestic labour, and temporary service organisations being provided during busy agricultural seasons (Thorborg 1978:540:48). These government directives, however, were never able to penetrate or adequately challenge the resistance of the traditional patriarchal organisation of kinship at the level of the lineage/family/household because there was continued economic incentive to maintain wealth within the patrilineal kin grouping. Womens' relation to production was weakened because the economic survival of the family depended on exogamously marrying women not being allowed to inherit property. In addition, although work point assessments varied over time and according to region, women generally received fewer work points than men irrespective of the accounting system employed. Women were supposed to receive equal pay if they completed the same number of tasks as men in a given period, but because of male kinship hegemony, were often given tasks with lower work point values, thereby receiving fewer points irrespective of the effort put into the task. Women also lost several days income during menstruation either because they were excused from work or not allowed to engage in agricultural labour. Women received less income as they worked a shorter day then men because of their domestic commitments. Communal service organisation which could have relieved women of their domestic burden was not a high priority for patrilineal clansmen because they invested through the bride price in women's capacity for productive and domestic labour (Diamond 1975:30) which structurally reinforced the prevailing modes of the organisation of work and kinship.

Although women were responsible for essential reproductive and domestic labour their position in society served to make males the most important workers to a lineage/family/household unit. This occurred because men had roots in the village/production teams, they earned a greater number of work points for more days per annum and they retired from productive labour later than women. The greater the importance of the role that men had in production generally, the more patrilineal kin groupings were strengthened, reinforcing inter-team/brigade/commune inequality through the retention of wealth for the family unit. Females in turn, facilitated the maintenance of males as high status producers and supported the unequal distribution of resources on the communes because they married out and could not claim family inheritance. They also helped to maintain the attendant rituals particular to Chinese kinship organisation such as ancestor worship, halls of ancestry and corporate lineages. Women therefore, retained an inferior position in their clan of birth as well as their adopted family upon marriage, while being simultaneously instrumental as the structural link in maintaining the prevailing combined modes of the patriarchal organisation of kinship, socialist semi-capitalist mode of the organisation of work and the Chinese mode of ethnicity.

The decline of the commune system and continued strengthening of patrilineal kinship organisation

National policies adopted by the recent government administration in China continue to strengthen patrilineal lineage/family/household ties and further weaken the position of women by emphasising the family unit as a socioeconomic unit of production. These recent reforms which have parallelled the decline of the commune system include implementation of a 'responsibility system'. According to this new system a group, family or individual is required to make a contract with the collective unit that specifies the amount to be produced from a permanently assigned piece of land. Productive work is remunerated according to short-term contract and contracted seasonal, specialised farm work.

Peasants under this system make an agreement with the production team to produce a specific quantity of crop or product and keep the remainder that is not retained by the collective. In South China, 70 per cent of houses engage in this type of family farming system, while the remainder works collectively in production teams and is allotted a portion of collective produce from communal labour. Work point schemes in general have changed nationwide from mutual assessment to payments for the actual work accomplished, which increases incentives for those who produce the largest amounts of crops or products. All work is performed for pecuniary reward and the government may no longer require any individual to work without monetary compensation. Families operating under the responsibility system are therefore liable for all costs and make all profits while the system continues to be partially based on the public ownership of land (Beijing Review 1982a:21-27).

There is increasing evidence that piece-rate payment for work as well as payment according to the amount of work performed may lead to greater income inequality and strengthen patrilocal residence and the inferior position of women because male able-bodied workers will continue to earn the highest incomes. Families with larger numbers of small children, elderly relatives or disabled members will suffer in relation to family households that contain more males who are able-bodied. Preference for male children is becoming even more pronounced as men continue to earn more because of women's irregular work patterns. With the economic responsibility system successful farmers in Guangdong province for example, are willing to pay the high cost of bearing children to reap the rewards of having extra labour. Sons are preferred because the sentiment of sons belonging to the natal family, while daughters belong to strangers remains strong in the countryside. This attitude is reflected by such practices as property continuing to be divided among the brothers and wife-beating by husbands and mothers-in-law if the wife bears a girl, especially in cases where the one child policy is operational (Wolf 1985:223, 257, 258-9). There are also signs that the traditional patterns of women as unpaid family workers may re-emerge under the family farming system, with the sexual division of labour intensifying. With work organised increasingly around the family unit women no longer have the labour protection that they experienced under the brigade level of the commune system. In the event that women are treated unfairly they will not report their male kin to the brigade level in areas where it continues to exist. Women have also lost in many cases their control over sideline production (Wolf 1985:268-69). The position of women is likely to deteriorate as women become confined to domestic labour in privatised family farming sectors and earn fewer work points in the collective sectors.

The inferior position of women is compounded by the fact that contract labour is divided according to specialised tasks, often on a permanent basis rather than in the form of job rotation. Assigning persons to specialised tasks will further the demise of the integration of mental and manual labour. Some families will perform menial mental tasks, such as carting manure, while others will be involved in more mentally rewarding jobs such as seed selection (Gittings 1981:5). Labour hierarchies are increasing which are linked to prosperous teams, with the educated and the technically learned at the top of the hierarchy and those performing menial tasks at the bottom of the production ladder. Women remaining in-marrying strangers are finding themselves at the lower end of the hierarchy, because although daughters are seen to benefit the family by earning points in the collective sector, they remain temporary members of the production teams who will not be given the best education and training (Nee 1981:32-40). Women in factories are becoming the last hired and first fired persons as factories seek high production rates. Women are the lowest paid workers and perform the most monotonous jobs. Discrimination against women is also becoming a regular feature of many occupations with women given less time for study and promotional opportunities (Wolf 1985:261-66).

Patrilineal kinship in the countryside is not being challenged directly by the present government administration. Instead, the communes have been divested of their political power while cadres are being replaced by township agents directly accountable to the centralised governing body of China. The government is using loyalty to patrilineal kin to encourage economic growth, while it is simultaneously attempting to weaken kinship networks through greater centralisation of political power. The peasantry is being encouraged to manage its own production and business affairs. There is an implied ideological emphasis being placed on individual family effort and hard work to produce wealth for the family/household unit, which also accumulates wealth for the social remains of the lineages. Government control, once exercised through cadres in the form of political ideology and directive is being replaced by economic incentives implemented by the township agents. In the latter manner, the government is gaining greater control over patrilineal kin groupings because they are able to reward particular regions or penalise others through the township agents (Lippit 1981:29). Definitive patterns showing how effective this policy will be on a nationwide basis and the extent to which township agents will be loyal to the government or as in traditional days favour their clansmen is not as yet known.

The government has attempted to use the incentives measure to implement a one child birth control policy, which could have marked long term effects on the position of women in Chinese society. Yangbei Production Brigade provides an example of incentives scheme, where sanctions have been applied if women refused to have the I.U.D. inserted after bearing two children. Families lost their rights to receive grain rations and a plot allotment on the birth of their third child. In a number of cases they were also required to open up one mu of land for cultivation. The burden of the third child not sanctioned by the government became so great that the majority of couples practiced birth control after the second child, instead of bearing the desired two boys and one girl. Families who volunteered to limit their progeny to two children, were rewarded with goods and money by the government. Government policy has been successful in limiting progeny to two, but mainly in cases of one child being male (Nee 1981:32-40). As noted in the wealthier region of Guangdong province, with the new responsibility system successful farmers are willing to pay the high cost of bearing additional children to gain the rewards of extra, especially male labour (Wolf 1985:257).

The recent population policy changes could facilitate the breakdown of the patriarchal organisation of kinship, but this is unlikely to occur because recent policies also reinforce patrilocal residence, income inequality and an inferior position for women in society. The one child per family policy coupled with the responsibility system could weaken the social remains of lineage kinship structure, by increasing substantially the importance of female children, establishing nuclear families and bringing in male sons-in-law. However, given the reinforcement of traditional patriarchal forms of the organisation of kinship, in terms of male biased inheritance and support for the elderly, the current pattern of behaviour tends towards couples becoming more resolute in their desire to have a greater number of children to ensure that a son is born to the household (Stacy 1983). The government facilitates this desire through such policies as giving a son's rations to his parents if he rejects his financial obligations to his parents (Wolf 1985:224). Families of more than one child occur throughout China and the resistance to the one child policy has been detrimental to females serving to foster wifebeating and the wilful neglect of daughters. Daughters are not being accepted as equals to sons and continue to be subject to the traditional abuse of female offspring.[2] Wife-beating continues to be prevalent in China and women are beaten in rural areas as noted, by both husbands and mothers-in-law if the only child to be born is a girl (Wolf 1985:235, 258-9). Crimes against women are increasing in general mainly in the family based forms of female infanticide, abuse of mothers with girl children, abduction, persecution and other forms of general abuse against women. The educational achievements of women are low, marriages continue to be arranged and heavy household chores ruin the health and progress of women. The most frequent quarrels within the family remain between mothers-in-law and daughters-in-law (Wolf 1985:230-3, 261-2).

It is doubtful that female offspring will be accepted as having the same worth as male children or that the one child birth control policy will prove workable while the patriarchal organisation of kinship is maintained with its attendant patrilineal inheritance and patrilocal residence. Smaller production teams and the emphasis on the individual family as an economic unit may weaken lineage solidarity because families within the lineage group may become economic competitors.[3] The government is allowing such economic competition to occur in encouraging a more consumer oriented society. Consequently, material inequalities are rising between and within communes, with some production teams/brigades/communes (or former ones) becoming prosperous while others remain relatively impoverished. The government is not intervening in these circumstances by distributing resources from the prosperous teams/brigades to the poorer ones to any great extent A number of less wealthy teams have been aided through annual investments and loans (Beijing Review 1982b: 18-26) but material inequality continues to rise and lineage solidarity remains strong, with some villages possessing watch towers because of cross-lineage feuding. This situation is largely a result, of the continuing contradiction between the government's stated goal of achieving a socialist organisation of work and its attempts on a practical level to implement policies that facilitate social relations belonging to the capitalist organisation of work.

The commune system is becoming an increasingly unworkable form of social organisation because families are being encouraged to pursue economic growth in their own individual districts, which inhibits lineage based teams from working on an inter-lineage commune level. Material inequality which is rising in the countryside is tending to strengthen the traditional, patriarchal organisation of kinship, reinforcing traditional roles for women, because female members are being pressured to preserve family inheritance through exogamous marriage. Women from less wealthy families/households are bearing the double burden of an inferior position in their natal and adopted families and poverty. The major protection that women may utilise to strengthen their position within the patrilineal family are the emotional bonds that they have created between themselves and their sons. Often this constitutes a fragile form of protection (Wolf 1985:11). The ideology of patriarchy remains strong in both substance and ritual, while the ideology of the commune is steadily weakening.

Re-integration into the world economic order

The weakening of the commune system within the organisation of work at the level of the nation, emanating from the bottom levels of the lineage/family/household of the organisation of kinship have affected Chinese foreign policy. The continuing patriarchal organisation of kinship coupled with a form of the state capitalist organisation of work and a Chinese mode of ethnicity is facilitating China's re-integration into the world economic order. Indicators of increasing dependency on Western nations, despite China's caution concerning the dangers of reproducing circumstances analogous to the encroachment of Western nations in the nineteenth century may be evidenced in the rise in trade relations between China and the West. Jia Shi, who has been the Chinese Vice-minister of Foreign Trade, pointed out in the journal China's Foreign Trade, that China's per annum foreign trade turnover of $14.8 billion in 1977, was doubled in 1980 to $36.6 billion not only because of economic recovery in China, but through the pursuit of the open-door economic policy (China Trade and Economic Newsletter 1981). Other forms of economic contact that portend increased links with the West and the possibility of greater dependency include the following policies;

1. Joint equity ventures that allow the foreign partners to have a majority holding. There is a possibility that this policy may lead to a situation reminiscent of the 1920's and 1930's, whereby Western business interests expanded into manufacturing, eventually controlling factories in China that produced a wide range of goods from bean oil to textiles. By the 1930's, over 40 per cent of all yarn spindles and 70 per cent of power looms in China were foreign owned (Business Strategies for the People's Republic of China 1980:2-3, Moulder 1977: 19-127).
2. Foreign component assembly and the purchasing of materials from foreign partners. In my estimation, there is a similarity and potential for the practice to develop along the lines of the railroad agreements made in the early 1900's. Foreign loans utilised to construct the railways had stipulations attached to them which required that construction materials were to be foreign bought, administration had to be at least partially foreign controlled, high percentage commission fees were to be charged for construction costs and that initial profits were utilised to repay the loan (Business Strategies for the People's Republic of China 1980:2-3; Moulder 1977:98-127).
3. Foreign participation in offshore oil production and exploration coupled with the increased use of international tender for contracts. This policy although employed to obtain Western technology could lead to the domination by foreign companies of energy resources of government projects, which was a situation that occurred at the turn of the century.
4. The establishment of organisations to attract investment capital from overseas Chinese and foreign firms (China Trade and Economic Newsletter 1981).

A number of internal economic reforms also reflect the increased Western contact and shift in industrialisation policies, they include:

1. The policy that allows provinces and municipalities to directly handle trade and business transactions with foreign

firms. This practice permits foreign firms to have contact with the interior of China and exposes it to foreign influence.

2. The policy that permits factories and other state enterprises, to keep a percentage of foreign exchange earnings, have a part in employee selection and firing, to procure supplies from the source of their choice according to market demands and to keep a percentage of profit to distribute to employees as bonuses, benefits or incentives (Business Strategies for the People's Republic of China 1980:2-3).

The failure of the Chinese to challenge the patrilineal organisation of kinship at the levels of the lineage/family/household hindered attempts to extricate China from the world economic order and the liberation of women from their inferior position in society. The patrilineal organisation of kinship has been traditionally so integrally linked to the organisation of work through patrilineal inheritance and exogamous marriage that to have challenged the economic functions of only the lineages was an inadequate measure because they remained social units based on related families/households which continued to be economic units of production. The peculiarities of the Chinese organisation of ethnicity also served to solidify the combined union of patrilineal kinship and feudal/budding capitalist organisation through corporate halls and ritual ancestor worship in general. The inferior position of women has been so integrally bound to these combined modes, based particularly within the organisation of kinship, that the facile challenging of this social order by the CCP and the commune system subsequently failed to deal with the multiplicity of linkages between the specific set of combined modes that maintained women in an inferior position in Chinese society.

Notes

1. Wolf and Witke, (1978:8-10), and mainly Topley, (1978:67-88), argue convincingly that marriage resistance occurred in the Canton Delta region among female silk workers unlike the Yangtze region because the Canton Delta produced more broods of silkworms annually, making greater labour demands on women; celibacy held a higher valuation because of it's association with dissident religious groups; girls' houses existed; sectarianism was strong and importantly; the large male migration to Southeast Asia required mothers and their children to be supported by the working daughter. Yet, these authors do not analyse the centrality of lineage and class in these circumstances which is a point criticised by Sankar.

2. Judith Stacy (1983) in her Epilog discusses how birth control policies could weaken lineage solidarity and subsequently affect the position of women. She does not forsee the one child family becoming a reality because of male elder opposition and the fact that the government is not as concerned with female equality as it is with population control.

   See Foreign Broadcast Information Service Daily Reports People's Republic of China, the latter part of 1982 and beginning of 1983 for reports of abuse of female children.

3. This idea occurred to me during an enlightening discussion with Professor William Parish at the American Sociological Association meeting, which took place in San Francisco in September 1982.

   Dr. Leslie Sklair was particularly helpful with information concerning his primary experience of the Chinese communes.

Concluding summary

In conclusion, the combination modes theory which encompasses the organisation of work, the organisation of kinship and the organisation of ethnicity has been utilised to elucidate the nature of social change in relation to historical development in developing societies. Women have been used as a vehicle to demonstrate how this theory may be utilised to explain the position of a segment of the community, region or nation within the context of historically specific social change irrespective of age or sex. Women were also viewed by the author as a necessary theoretical device to show that in the bulk of the literature dealing with social change and historical development it is assumed that men are the main focus of such enquiries. Women tend to be presented, as are children, as a peripheral part of the organisation of the structures of society except within the limited context of the household and family. The household and family levels of analysis are both underemphasised in the male oriented world systems, dependency, modernisation or other economic based analyses of developing societies, while they are overstressed in feminist accounts. The latter tends to underestimate the importance of the economy as a whole and the position of men both within and without the organisation of kinship. Both imbalanced emphases on either the organisation of work or the organisation of kinship overlook the important structural linkages that cross modes, the different levels of analyses and the age and sex of the individuals. Social change therefore, may affect any particular segment of the society under observation from the top down of the world economic order level of society or the bottom up from the family/household level of society.

In addressing the linkages and dynamic nature of social change which may be initiated or hindered at any level within any combination of given modes, all social actors in society are viewed as dynamic beings who react to changing social structures. No group of social actors regardless of age or sex are perpetually subordinate or dominant to another in any given society as a dialectical relationship exists between all dominant and subordinate groups and between combination modes. In one case, the organisation of kinship may be the dominant mode in shaping the other two modes or two may be stronger while the other one is weaker in influence. Women as a social group are often portrayed as helpless 'victims' who are perpetually subordinate to men or an international capitalist class universally. Women in different societies, as shown in the case studies, are not helpless victims, but resist suppression and use societal institutions for their own ends and needs. The Chinese and Israeli Kibbutz case studies were examples of women using such social institutions as the family to resist male dominance and authority and to gain power and status in society. The Malaysian case illustrated how younger women in particular have taken advantage of the opportunities presented to them in work and education to gain greater freedom and earn wages higher than their male relatives.

Finally, the combination modes theory which has drawn it's perspective from a number of theories as noted in the review and criticism in Chapter One, has attempted to avoid ethnocentric appraisals of other, especially non-Western societies and the tendency to generalise on a universal basis.

The combination modes theory provides a flexible analysis at numerous levels of social organisation which allows it to appraise historically specific produced circumstances that give rise to a particular structure of society at any given historical period. The different modes combine in a specific manner to produce a set of modes such a patriarchal capitalist Chinese or bilineal/patriarchal capitalist Malaysian, unique to a particular nation, ethnic group or tribe at any given historical period. This approach avoids universal generalisations that depart from empiricism to the extent that theory becomes divorced from reality.

Ethnocentric analysis both generalises and obscures reality because the context of the enquiry is within the enquirer's own cultural framework. Modernisation theory applies Western definitions of modernity to 'traditional' societies without analysing how indigenous social organisations function to sustain efficiently the social fabric of those societies. 'Pre-modern' societies because they are not Western are deemed unprogressive and backward, and in need of a new, advanced social structure based on Western society. Feminist theorists also impute generalised concepts based on their Western societal experiences onto women in developing societies. They universalise such ideas as patriarchy, which they do not define clearly, and argue that it is the major cause of the universal subordination of women. World system/dependency theorists argue ethnocentrically that Western nations are the 'centre' or 'core' of a generalised world system. All change in developing societies is initiated by Western nations creating eventually a uniform Western capitalist world system. In a few cases where connections between the world economic order, nation state and household are acknowledged, the multiplicity and complexities of linkages are overlooked with social change derived only from a Western centered world economic system.

The combination modes theory therefore addresses the theoretical weaknesses of lack of historical specificity, depth of analysis, polemics in terms of one group deemed the subordinate victim and the other the dominant enemy, ethnocentrism, the tendency to universalise generalisations and a lack of neutrality in analytical categories. The application of the combination modes theory to a number of different, empirically based case studies has both put forward this alternative and complementary theoretical analysis and addressed such weaknesses as outlined above through a different combination modes based emphasis.

In relation to the current changing situation in Malaysia because of the recent introduction of world market factories the combination modes theory allows us to analyse how these social changes are rooted historically in socioeconomic change initiated within the organisation of work at the level of the world economic order and how men, women and children were affected within the organisation of kinship at the level of the family. The recent introduction of world market factories such as electronics component manufacture has initiated change in the structure of the Malaysian family affecting members according to age and sex. Because of this historically specific analysis at a multiplicity of levels and linkages, we found that daughters were affected by this social change in particular and in relation to the organisation of ethnicity that it was Malay women of the three main ethnic groups in Malaysia, who are preferred by electronics factories.

In the case of contemporary Malaysia, social change has been initiated from the top down level of the world economic order affecting both the organisation of ethnicity and kinship.

In the case of the Kibbutz, social change is occurring at the levels of the family and ethnic group within the organisation of kinship and ethnicity respectively. Dissatisfaction at the family level within the organisation of kinship is linked to the traditional mode of ethnicity which gave women their status and power within the family context. The Jewish structure of the family brought from Eastern and Central Europe and more recently Middle Eastern and Southern European countries was never fully challenged. This was compounded by the fact that at the community level of the organisation of work women were never fully integrated into social production and men did not seriously partake in the service sectors. The linkages between the combination modes have shown how women and men have remained divided within the Kibbutz community despite the rights of women being among the most extensive of any society on a worldwide basis. Social change on the Kibbutzim, although initiated originally by national strivings to regain an historical homeland at the level of the nation, within the mode of ethnicity is now being instigated by women at the level of the family. Change is therefore being initiated from the bottom up of the Kibbutz system at the level of the family within the organisation of kinship. Such change is drawing the Kibbutz network closer to Israel at the level of the nation state and the world economic order in the framework of market forces and the introduction of new capitalist technologies within the organisation of work.

The case of the Chinese commune has demonstrated that although change may be initiated from the top down because of Western encroachment through trading practices at the level of the world economic order within the organisation of work, the family can be a reservoir of resistance to such change. The organisation of kinship within the Chinese case at the levels of the lineage/family/household which were in historical tradition integrally linked to one another, has been such a powerful structure in the Chinese countryside that after reshaping itself with the advent of the commune system, it reformulated once more into a strong unit. The lineage/family/household as a unit served to erode the commune system at the level of the nation within the organisation of work giving rise to a semi-state capitalist-socialist system and re-incorporating China to an extent into the world economic order. The organisation of ethnicity within the context of rituals, customs and language in relation to the maintenance of the corporate lineage and extended family kept the lineage/family/household unit strong, helping to undermine the limited challenge to the corporate lineage by the CCP. The combination modes theory allowed us to analyse how social change occurred from the top down exacerbating internal foment and giving rise to the commune system, and then from the bottom up during the commune period which was the focus of our examination. It also showed how women were the inferior, yet essential structural links who through their reproductive capacity kept lineage/family/household wealth and inheritance within patrilineal clan groups.

The three case studies further demonstrated how women are not passive victims, perpetually subordinate to men in a universal, ahistorical manner.

Within the Malaysian context women are using their new found status as wage earners to gain independence and status within the family and village community. While many men remain unemployed or underemployed, unable to find work in the villages or urban centres, female family members, daughters in particular, often obtain relatively high paid employment as production workers in electronics plants. Women electronics production workers are in contact with another culture, Western culture, and they are gaining experience in industry, which the Malaysian government views as the primary sector to cultivate in the course of their capitalist industrialisation plans. Instead of being passive victims, Malay women are choosing to avail themselves of the opportunites presented by electronics factory manufacture.

Women are also not passive victims in the case of the Kibbutz system and as noted experience a good deal of independence compared to many other societies. Dissatisfaction with their work or with the greater choice they believe women in non-Kibbutz society have achieved, has caused Sabra women to demand and obtain some significant internal changes. Dissatisfied with their position they are not passively acquiescing to the demands of men, but are pursuing greater change. They have demanded greater professional training and status, greater consumer choice and family sleeping, which they have obtained in varying degrees according to the particular Kibbutz movement. Women of the Kibbutz movement are derived historically from pioneering women who fought for every right they gained and most difficult was the initial right to immigrate to Palestine to establish Kibbutzim.

Women in the Chinese case have had a more difficult experience in resisting against their structurally enforced passivity within the Chinese system. Burdened by thousands of years of traditional exogamous marriage within close patrilineal clans and subjugation within the family to all male members and mothers-in-law, suffering bound feet and holding an inferior position within religious ideology, the majority of Chinese women had the greatest tendency to be passive victims. However, even in the most traditional of circumstances women did resist historically by committing suicide if they became too oppressed by other family members or they resisted marriage when they gained independent earning status in the case of the Canton silkworkers in the early twentieth century. During the rise of the CCP and throughout the commune period women were active despite the lingering persistence of the idea that they should hold a passive, inferior place in society and the continuation of exogamous marriage into patrilineal clans. Women also organised women's associations, to support women and draw attention to family centered abuse against women and to apply group pressure upon men who continued to beat their wives. Women were active in agricultural labour and were presented as model all-female teams in some cases. In the traditional family context women were not passive, utilising every avenue of power they could exploit. Women oppressed brutally other women in their capacities as mothers-in-law, most particularly their daughters-in-law. They ensured that their sons became emotionally attached to them rather than their wives in order to manipulate male power to further their own ends. Wives of the landlord class lineages were even more fierce according to Hinton (1966) in defense of family wealth than were male family members; preferring to see their children tortured rather than reveal the hiding place that contained family wealth. Chinese women in general fought hard, when allowed the opportunity, during the rise of the CCP to improve their position within the family and society, which is the reason that they felt great victory once they had gained a societally sanctioned voice within the family, especially as young brides, earning work points and wages.

Ethnocentric bias and the tendency to universalise is another area of analysis that the combination modes thesis has addressed. In the Malaysian case attempts to overcome ethnocentric bias and generalisations have been made by assessing the historically specific conditions that gave rise to the current position of women and the nature of the different cultures in Malaysia. In relation to the organisation of kinship the bilineal roots of Malayan families gave rise to economically active female family members who also exercised a high degree of independence. Patriarchal tendencies introduced during the period of Islamic Conquest, invested the father with greater authority, but did little to diminish the egalitarian nature of the bilineal foundation of the Malayan family. The high economic activity of Malay women derived from their independent, traditional roles as managers and those in charge of family finances explained why their entrance into the colonial opium manufacturing, rubber tapping and electronics industries was a relatively smooth transition at the level of the community within the organisation of work. Internal features indigenous to Malay culture were assessed in their own terms within the mode of ethnicity rather than through Western interpretation or practice. For example, the hysteria which Malay women production workers exhibit when placed under severe production quota pressure is related to their religion and cultural ideas of socially acceptable ways to express anger. The deferential and modest behaviour exhibited by Malayan women electronics production workers is also cultural in nature rather than gender based as feminists would argue in relation to their ideas of the universal subordination of women. Malayan and other Southeast Asian women are preferred workers in such world market factories as electronics because of the combination of a number of factors within the different modes including; their high historical economic activity, their gender socialisation in the family which trains them for delicate tasks, their cultural training in modesty and deference to authority coupled with their being a relatively cheap source of labour. Such historically specific analysis challenges the externally imposed explanations of the modernisation and world systems/dependency theorists who tend to view the developing world as a uniform whole that is shaped by the progressive Western nations having no history or unique qualities of their own. The Malay nation is not a static society being totally drained of all it's resources, but is benefitting to an extent in terms of revenue, employment and technology as are Malay women in electronics factories who are earning relatively high wages. The exchange therefore between Western nations and Malaya is not completely unequal or shaped solely by the former, as the latter not only gains to a certain extent, but also shapes conditions in the West as it's unique combination of modes provides Western based manufacturing firms with required needs.

The Kibbutz provides such a unique experiment both socially and ethnically that generalisations or ethnocentric bias would only lead to a grossly misinterpreted viewpoint. The combination modes thesis has circumvented ethnocentricity and universalistic conclusions through analysing the historical roots of the Kibbutz movement which lay in the aspirations of the Jewish people to return to their ancient homeland. This very specific historically based ambition coupled with the experience of the Jewish people in Russia and their contact with the form of socialism espoused by the Russian intelligensia gave rise to ideas of agricultural collectives in the ancient land of Israel. The young pioneers wished to escape the oppressiveness of the traditional Jewish family although women had a very clearly defined and important role within the organisation of kinship at the level of the family. Young Jewish men rejected the limited range of occupations open to them through discriminatory laws imposed on them in host countries. They wished to return to the land, moving away from business and commerce, to establish a socialist mode of work at the level of the community. All pioneers were also motivated by their desire to live a Jewish life in freedom away from the persecution and constraints of their host nations. The Jewish mode of ethnicity at the level of the ethnic group was therefore a central factor in the desires of the young pioneers to establish Kibbutzim. In the religious collectives, Judaism as a religion rather than solely an identity played a central role in the lives of the members.

To understand the present day dissatisfaction of many women of the Kibbutz movement with their relegation to the service sectors and their limited roles in family life, historical specific factors of women's relative exclusion from social production, their loss of individual status with the collectivisation of housework, coupled with their history of strong roles within the traditional Jewish family has required analysis. Socio-biological generalisations that are based on a purported intrinsic universal nature of men and women or feminist assertions that all women need to be freed from family ties do not address the historical specifics of the particular ethnic experience of the Jewish people who initiated and continue to be a part of the Kibbutz movement or the combination of circumstances that have caused women to become dissatisfied with their lives.

The Chinese commune occurred during a specific point of Chinese history and was a result of circumstances extraordinary to Chinese society. Western nations attempted to colonise China, but failed because of it's vastness and the insular, suspicious attitudes of the populace towards foreigners, and were only able to create spheres of influence. Consequently, it is futile to make broad generalisations about the communes and why they occurred or to view China in terms of being a peripheral part of the world system and dependent on the West is to oversimplify a complex enquiry. The combination modes thesis serves to underscore this complexity in allowing an analysis of how both external and internal factors within the organisation of work combined at all levels, the world economic order, nation state and community, to destabilise Chinese society before the advent of the commune system. At the level of the world economic order, Western encroachment reversed China's strong trading position weakening the social order, while at the level of the nation state, warlords and corrupt government administrators were causing rapid internal decay. The community was also disintegrating because of internal strife, opium addiction, banditry and increased feuding between lineages. Worldwide depression accelerated this process and the collapse of the social order gave rise to the CCP and the commune system. The organisation of kinship, at all three levels of the lineage, family and household, was the foundation of conservatism in the countryside, maintaining women in an inferior position. Kinship relations at the levels of the family/household were consolidated by the lineage or extended family systems which formed small, powerful social units within the community. Rituals and customs within the Chinese organisation of ethnicity served to legitimise religiously the power of the lineages/extended families through ancestor worship and religious ceremony. This cultural dimension strengthened the lineage/extended family/household in the countryside also supporting patriliny and exogamous marriage because of the predominance of the patriarchal mode of organisation. Women therefore, because of the strength of the patrilineal clan system and their role as structural links between the organisations of work, kinship and ethnicity had little lattitude for change. They remained essential structural links for the reproduction of male children to further the male line, retain inherited wealth for patrilineal kin and as socialisers of children in rearing them in traditional Chinese custom and ritual. These combined modes peculiar to the Chinese case maintained women in an inferior position and weakened the commune system.

In conclusion, the combination modes thesis is an attempt to provide a theory to explain historical development within a framework that is applicable to any culture under observation. Cross-cultural analysis presents many difficulties because the social organisation of each society is structured differently according to the constitution of it's modes of kinship, work and ethnicity. Rather than making universalistic generalisations or inappropriate statistical comparisons, a neutral set of categories that allows the same dimensions of each society to be analysed in it's own terms is apposite for cross-cultural analysis. The combination modes thesis is based in the historical specifics of each society while linking those specifics to external societal influences. It is also a theory that may be applied to all persons irrespective of age or sex in a neutral manner.

References

References - Chapter One

Al-Hibri, A. 'Capitalism is an Advanced Stage of Patriarchy: But Marxism is Not Feminism', in L. Sargent (ed) Women and Revolution (Boston 1981).

Anglade, C. and C. Fortin (ed) The State and Capital Accumulation in Latin America, Volume I (London 1985).

Anthias, F. and N. Yuval-Davis 'Contextualizing feminism-gender, ethnic class divisions' Feminist Review, No.15 1983.

Amin, S. Accummulation on a World Scale: a Critique of the Theory of Underdevelopment (New York 1975).

Amin, S. 'Accummulation and Development: a Theoretical Model', Review of African Political Economy, Volume I 1974.

Amos, V. and P. Parmar 'Challenging Imperial Feminism' Feminist Review No.17 Many Voices, One Chant: Black Feminist Perspectives 1984.

Arizpe, L. 'Women in the Informal Labour Sector: the case of Mexico City', in Wellesley Editorial Committee (ed) Women and National Development: The Compexities of Change (Chicago 1977).

Atkinson, T. Amazon Odyssey (New York 1974).

Bandarage, A. 'Women in Development: Liberalism, Marxism and Marxist-Feminism', Development and Change, Volume 15, 1984.

Barrett, M. Women's Oppression Today (London 1980).

Barrett, M. and M. McIntosh The Anti-social Family (London 1982)

Beechey, V. 'On Patriarchy' Feminist Review, No.3 1979.

Bendix, R. 'Tradition and Modernity Reconsidered' in R. Bendix Embattled Reason (New York 1970).

Beneria, L. Women and Development, the Sexual Division of Labour in Rural Societies (New Jersey 1982).

Bennholdt-Thomson, V. 'Subsistence production and extended reproduction' in K. Young, C. Wolkowitz, R. McCullagh (ed) Of Marriage and the Market (London 1984).

Benston, M. 'The Political Economy of Women's Liberation', Monthly Review Volume 21, No.4 1969.

Bloch, M. and J. Bloch 'Women and the dialectics of nature in eighteenth-century French thought' in C. MacCormack and M. Strathern (ed) Nature, Culture and Gender (Cambridge 1980).

Booth, D. 'Marxism and development sociology: Interpreting the impasse', World Development Volume 13, No.7 1985.

Boserup, E. Women's Role in Economic Development (New York 1970).

Bourguignon, E. (ed) A World of Women: Anthropological Studies of Women in Societies of the World (New York 1980).

Bradby, B. 'The destruction of the natural economy' Economy and Society Volume 26, No.2 1978.

Brenner, R. 'The Origins of Capitalist Development: a Critique of Neo-Smithian Maxism' New Left Review September-October 1977.

Buhk, J. 'Women in subsistence production in Ghana' in Women in rural development-critical issues (Geneva 1980).

Carby, H. 'White woman listen! Black feminism and the boundaries of sisterhood' in Centre for Contemporary Cultural Studies 1982.

Cardoso, F.H. and E. Faletto, Dependency and Development in Latin America (Berkeley 1979).

Chinchilla, N. 'Industrialisation, Monopoly Capitalism and Women's Work in Guatemala' in Wellesley Editorial Committee (ed) Women and National Development: The Complexities of Change (Chicago 1977).

Chipp, S. and J. Green (ed) Asian Women in Transition (Pennsylvania 1980).

Chodorow, N. Mothering: Psychoanalysis and the Social Organization of Gender (Berkeley 1978).

Chodorow, N. 'Family Structure and Feminine Personality' in M. Rosaldo and L. Lamphere (ed) Women, Culture and Society (Stanford 1974).

Clignet, R. 'Social Change and Sexual Differentiation in the Cameroun and Ivory Coast' in Wellesley Editorial Committee (ed) Women and National Development: The Complexities of Change (Chicago 1977).

Cole, J. 'Women in Cuba: The Revolution Within the Revolution' in B. Lindsay (ed) Comparative Perspectives of Third World Women: The Impact of Race, Sex and Class (New York 1980).

Collier, J. 'Women in Politics' in M. Rosaldo and L. Lamphere (ed) Women, Culture and Society (Stanford 1974).

Collver, H. and E. Langlois 'The Female Labor Force in Metropolitan Areas: an International Comparison' Economic Development and Cultural Change Volume 10, No.4 1962.

Dalla Costa, M. and S. James The Power of Women and the Subversion of the Community (London 1975).

De Beauvoir, S. The Second Sex (New York 1952).

Deere, C. 'Rural Women's Subsistence Production in the Capitalist Periphery' The Review of Radical Political Economics Volume 8, No.1 1976.

Delphy, C. The Main Enemy: A Materialist Analysis of Women's Oppression (London 1977).

Dixon-Mueller, R. Women's Work in Third World Agriculture, ILO (Geneva 1985).

Dixon, R. Rural Women at Work (John Hopkins 1978).

Edholm, F., O. Harris and K. Young 'Conceptualizing Women' Critique of Anthropology Volume 3 No. 9/10 1977.

Eisenstadt, S. 'Modernisation, Growth and Diversity' in S. Eisenstadt (ed) Tradition, Change and Modernity (New York 1973)

Eisenstein, Z. The Radical Future of Liberal Feminism (New York 1981).

Eisenstein, Z. 'Developing a Theory of Capitalist Patriarchy' in Eisenstein, Z. (ed) Capitalist Patriarchy and the Case for Socialist Feminism (New York 1979, 1978).

Elson, D. and R. Pearson 'Nimble Fingers Make Cheap Workers: An Analysis of Women's Employment in Third World Export Manufacturing' Feminist Review No.7 1981.

Elster, J. Ulysses and the Sirens (Cambridge 1979).

Engels, F. Origin of the Family, Private Property and the State (New York 1972).

Engels, F. The Condition of the Working Class in England (Stanford 1968).

Epstein, S. and R. Watts (ed) The Endless Day: Some Case Material on Asian Rural Women in Development (Oxford 1981).

Epstein, S. 'Planning with rural women', Special issue of Assignment Children, UNICEF, Geneva April-June 1977.

Erlich, C. 'The Unhappy Marriage of Marxism and Feminism; Can It Be Saved' in L Sargent (ed) Women and Revolution (Boston 1981).

Etienne, M. and E. Leacock Women and Colonization; Anthropological Perspectives (New York 1980).

Firestone, S. The Dialectic of Sex (New York 1970).

Folbre, N. and A. Ferguson 'The Unhappy Marriage of Patriarchy and Capitalism' in L. Sargent (ed) Women and Revolution (Boston 1981).

Frank, A. 'Dependence is Dead, Long Live Dependence and Class Struggle: A Reply to Critics' Latin American Perspectives Volume 1, No.1 1974.

Frank, A. Lumpenbourgeoisie: Lumpendevelopment-Dependence, Class and Politics in Latin America (New York 1972).

Freidan, B. The Feminine Mystique (London 1967).

Friedl, E. Women and Men; an anthropologists view (New York 1975).

Friedl, E. 'The position of women: appearance and reality' Anthropology Quarterly Volume 40 1967.

Geertz, C. The Interpretation of Culture (New York 1973).

Gidden, A. A Contemporary Critique of Historical Materialism (London 1982).

Gonzales, S. 'La Chicana: Guadalupe or Malinche' in B. Lindsay (ed) Comparative Perspectives of Third World Women; The Impact of Race, Sex and Class (New York 1980).

Goody, J. 'Uniqueness in the Cultural Conditions for Political Development in Black Africa' in S. Eisenstadt and S. Rokkan (ed) Building States and Nations (Beverly Hills 1973).

Gough, K. The Origin of the Family (London 1961)

Hammond, P. and A. Jablow Women: their economic role in traditional societies (Massachusetts 1973).

Harding, S. 'First Division of Labour Maintains Patriarchy and Capital' in L. Sargent Women and Revolution (Boston 1981).

Harris, O. 'The power of signs: gender, culture and the wild inthe Bolivian Andes' in C. MacCormack and M Strathern Nature, Culture and Gender (Cambridge 1980).

Hartmann, H. 'The Unhappy Marriage of Marxism and Feminism: Towards a More Progressive Union' in L. Sargent Women and Revolution (Boston 1981).

Hartmann, H. 'The Unhappy Marriage of Marxism and Feminism: Toward a More Progressive Union' Capital and Class No. 8 Summer 1979.

Hartmann, H. 'Capitalism, Patriarchy and Job Segregation by Sex' SIGNS 1 1976.

Humphries, J. 'Class Struggle and the Persistence of the Working Class Family' Cambridge Journal of Economics 1 1977.

Huston, P. Third World Women Speak Out (New York 1979).

Inkeles, A. 'Making Men Modern: on the Causes and Consequences of Individual Change in Six Developing Countries' American Journal of Sociology 75 1969.

Jeffreys, P. Frogs in a Well (London 1980).

Jordonova, L.J. 'Natural facts: a historical perspective on science and sexuality' in C. MacCormack and M. Strathern Nature, Culture and Gender (Cambridge 1980).

Joseph , G. 'The Incompatible Menage a Trois: Marxism, Feminism and Racism' in L. Sargent (ed) Women and Revolution (Boston 1981).

Kahl, J. The Measurement of Modernization: A Study of Values in Brazil and Mexico (Texas 1968).

Kandiyotti, D. 'Sex Roles and Social Change: A Comparative Appraisal of Turkey's Women' in Wellesley Editorial Committee (ed) Women and National Development: The Complexities of Change (Chicago 1977).

King, M. 'Cuba's Attack on Women's Second Shift 1974-1976' Latin American Perspectives Volume 4 No.1, 2 1977.

Lahav, P. 'Raising the Status of Women through Laws, the Case of Israel' in Wellesley Editorial Committee (ed) Women and National Development: The Complexities of Change (Chicago 1977).

Latin American and Caribbean Women's Collective Slaves of Slaves The Challenge of Latin American Women (London 1980).

Leavitt, R. 'Women in other Cultures' in V. Gornick and B. Moran (ed) Women and Sexist Society (New York 1972).

Levi-Strauss, C. 'The Family' in H. Shapiro (ed) Man, Culture and Society (Oxford 1971).

Leghorn, L. and K. Parker Woman's Worth, Sexual Economics and the World of Women (Boston 1981).

Leon de Leal, M. and C. Deere 'The Study of rural women and the development of capitalism in Columbian agriculture' Women in rural development: critical issues (Geneva 1980).

Lindsay, B. 'Introduction' in B. Lindsay (ed) Comparative Perspectives of Third World Women: The Impact of Race, Sex and Class (New York 1980).

Loutfi, M. Rural Women-Equal Partners in Development (Geneva 1980).

Marx, K. 'The Eighteenth Brumaire of Louis Bonaparte' in K. Marx and F. Engels Selected Works in Three Volumes Volume 1 (Moscow 1969).

MacCormack, C. 'Biological Events and Cultural Control' in Wellesley Editorial Committee (ed) Women and National Development: The Complexities of Change (Chicago 1977).

McIntosh, M. 'Gender and economics: the sexual division of labour and the subordination of women' in K. Young, C. Wolkowitz, R. McCullagh (ed) Of Marriage and the Market (London 1984)

Meillassoux, C. Femmes, greniers et capitaux (Paris 1975).

Meillassoux, C. 'From reproduction to production' Economy and Society 1, 1972.

Miles, R. Racism and Migrant Labour (London 1982).

Miles R. and A. Phizacklea Labour and Racism (London 1980).

Millet, K. Sexual Politics (New York 1970).

Miranda, G. 'Women's Labour Force Participation in a Developing Society: The Case of Brazil' in Wellesley Editorial Committee (ed) Women and World Development: The Complexities of Change (Chicago 1977).

Mitchell, J. The Longest Revolution (New York 1974).

Mitchell, J. Women's Estate (London 1971).

Molyneux, M. 'Family Reform in Socialist States: The Hidden Agenda' Feminist Review No.21 Winter 1985.

Molyneux, M. 'Socialist Policies Old and New: Progress Towards Women's Emancipation?' Feminist Review No.8 1981.

Molyneux, M. 'Women's Emancipation Under Socialism: A model for the Third World' Paper presented at the Development Studies Association, Swansea September 1980.

Myrdal, A. and V. Klein Women's Two Roles (London 1959).

Nash, J. 'Introduction' in J. Nash and H. Safa (ed) Sex and Class in Latin America (New York 1980).

Nelson, N. Why has Development Neglected Rural Women? A Review of the South Asian Literature (Oxford 1979).

Nelson, C. 'Public and Private Politics: Women in the Middle Eastern World' American Ethnologist 1, 3, 1974.

Oakley, A. Sex, Gender and Society (London 1972).

Ortner, S. 'Is Female to Male as Nature is to Culture? Feminist Studies 1, 2, 1972.

Papanek, H. 'Development Planning for Women: the implications of women's work' in R. Jahan and H. Papanek (ed) Women and Development: Perspectives from South and Southeast Asia (Dacca 1979).

Phelps, L. 'Patriarchy and Capitalism' Quest 1981.

Poewe, K. Matrilineal Ideology: Male-Female Dynamics in Luapula Zambia (London 1981).

Poulantzas, N. Political Power and Social Classes State Power and Socialism (London 1978).

Poulantzas, N. 'Internationalization of capitalist relations and the nation state' Economy and Society 3, 4, 1974.

Quinn, N. 'Anthropological Studies on Women's Status' Annual Review of Anthropology 6, 1977.

Rapp, R. 'Review Essay Anthropology' SIGNS 4,3, 1979.

Rey, P. 'The Lineage Mode of Production' Critique of Anthropology 3, 1975.

Rogers, B. The Domesticiation of Women: Discrimination in Developing Societies (London 1980).

Rosaldo, M. and L. Lamphere (ed) Women, Culture and Society (Stanford 1974).

Rothstein, F. Three Different Worlds Women, Men and Children in an Industrializing Community (Westport, Ct. 1982).

Rowbotham, S., L. Segal and H. Wainwright Beyond the Fragments: Feminism and the Making of Socialism (London 1980).

Rowbotham, S. Women, Resistance and Revolution (London 1974).

Rubin, G. 'The Traffic in Women' in R. Reiter (ed) Toward an Anthropology of Women (New York 1975).

Sacks, K. 'Engels revisited: women the organization of production and private property' in R. Reiter (ed) Towards an Anthropology of Women (New York 1975).

Saffioti, H. 'Female Labour and Capitalism in the United States and Brazil in R. Leavitt (ed) Women Cross-culturally: change and challenge (The Hague 1975).

Sanday, P. Female Power and Male Dominance (Cambridge 1981).

Sanday, P. 'Female Status in the Public Domain' in M. Rosaldo and L. Lamphere (ed) Women, Culture and Society (Stanford 1974).

Savane, M 'Women and rural development in Africa' in Women in rural development: critical issues (Geneva 1980).

Schneider, D. and K. Gough (ed) Matrilineal Kinship (Berkeley 1967).

Sharma, U. Women, Work and Property in North-West India (London 1980).

Sklair L. 'Transcending the Impasse, Metatheory and Empirical Research in the Sociology of Development and Underdevelopment', World Development, Volume 16, No.6, 1988.

Smith, J., I. Wallerstein and H. Evers Households and the World Economy (Beverly Hills 1984).

Stoler, A. 'Class Structure and Female Autonomy in Rural Java' in Wellesley Editorial Committee (ed) Women in National Development: The Complexities of Change (Chicago 1977).

Stolcke, V. 'Women's labours: the naturalisation of social inequality and women's subordination' in K. Young, C. Wolkowitz, R. McCullagh (ed) of Marriage and the Market (London 1984).

Sullerot, E. Women, Society and Change (New York 1971).

Taplin, R. 'Women as Marginal Social Actors, The Case of Economic Development' Journal of Interdisciplinary Economics Volume 3, No.1 1989.

Taplin, R. (ed) Special Issue on Development Journal of Interdicip-linary Economics. Forthcoming 1989.

Taplin, R. Women and World Development: a critique of the sociology of development unpublished PhD thesis (The London School of Economics 1984).

Tinker, I. and Bramsen M. (ed) Women and World Development (Washington D.C. 1976).

Thompson, E.P. The Making of the English Working Class (London 1963).

Towner, M. 'Monopoly Capitalism and Women's Work during the Porfiriato' Latin American Perspectives, 4 1977.

Wadley, S. 'Women and Hindu Tradition' in Wellesley Editorial Committee (ed) Women and National Development: The Complexities of Change (Chicago 1977).

Wallerstein, I. The Modern World System-Capitalist Agriculture and the Origins of European World Economy in the 16th Century (London 1974).

Wallerstein, I. 'Dependence in an Interdependent World: The Limited Possibilities of Transformation within the Capitalist World Economy' African Studies Review 17, 1 1974.

Wallerstein, I. 'Rise and Future Demise of the World Capitalist System: Concepts for Comparative Analysis' Comparative Studies of Society and History 10, 1974.

Ward, K. Women in the World Economic System (New York 1984).

Warren, B. Imperialism, Pioneer of Capitalism (New York 1980).

Weinbaum, B. Curious Courtship of Socialism and Women's Liberation (New York 1978).

Weinbaum, B. and A. Bridges 'The Other Side of the Paycheck: Monopoly Capital and Structure of Consumption' in Z. Eisenstein (ed) Capitalist Patriarchy and the Case for Socialist Feminism (New York 1979).

Weiner, M. Modernization, The Dynamics of Growth (New York 1966).

Whyte, M. The Status of Women in Pre-industrial Societies (Princeton 1978).

Wilensky, H. 'Women's Work, Economic Growth, Ideology and Social Structure' Industrial Relations 7, 3, 1968.

Wood, R. 'The Future of Modernization' in M. Weiner (ed) Modernization, the Dynamics of Growth (New York 1966).

Youssef, N. Women and Work in Developing Societies Population Monograph Series No.15 Berkeley 1974.

Zaretsky, E. Capitalism, the Family and Personal Life (London 1976).

Zeidenstein, S. and T. Abdullah 'Women's Reality: Critical Issues for Program Design' Studies in Family Planning No.10 1979.

References - Chapter Two

Asian Employment Programme, Employment and Labour Force in Asia, International Labor Organisation (Geneva 1980).

Boserup, E. Women's role in economic development (New York 1970).

Cardoso, F. and E. Faletto Dependency and Development in Latin America (Berkeley 1979).

Djamour, J. 'Malay Kinship and Marriage in Singapore' London School of Economics Monographs on Social Anthropology 21 (London 1959).

Elson, D. and R. Pearson 'Nimble fingers make cheap workers: An analysis of women's employment in Third World export manufacturing' Feminist Review (Spring 1981).

Emmanuel, A. Unequal Exchange: A Study of the Imperialism of Trade (New York 1972).

Firth, R. Housekeeping among Malay peasants (London 1966).

Frobel, F., J. Heinrichs and O. Kreye The New International Division of Labor (Cambridge 1980).

Fuentes, A. and B. Ehrenreich Women in the Global Factory (Boston 1983).

Global Electronics Issue No.88 November 1988 (Pacific Studies Center).

Grossman, R. 'Women's Place in the Integrated Circuit' Southeast Asian Chronicle No.66 1979.

Heyser, N. 'From Rural Subsistence to an Industrial Peripheral Work Force: An Examination of Female Malaysian Migrants and Capital Accumulation in Singapore' in L. Beneria (ed) Women and Development: The Sexual Division of Labor in Rural Economics (New York 1982).

Jamilah, M.A. 'Industrial Development in Peninsular Malaysia and rural migration of women workers: Impact and Implications' Jurnal Ekonomi Malaysia No.1 1980(a).

Jamilah, M.A. 'The position of women workers in the manufacturing industries in Malaysia', Penang, Malaysia: Consumers' Association of Penang, Seminar on Economics, Development and the Consumer November 1980(b).

Lau, E. 'Why Miss Free Trade Zone is a soft touch' The Guardian March 4, 1981.

Lim, L. 'Women in the Singapore Economy' Economic Research Centre, Occasional Paper Series No.5, National University of Singapore 1984.

McLellan, S. 'Reciprocity or Exploitation? Mothers and Daughters in the Changing Economy of Rural Malaysia' Working Papers on Women in International Development, Michigan State University, No.93, 1985.

Moulder, F. Japan, China and the Modern World Economy-Towards a re-interpretation of East Asian development ca.1600 to ca.1918 (Cambridge 1977).

New Straits Times, Monday 31st 1981.

Ong, A. 'Global industries and Malay peasants in peninsular Malaysia' in J. Nash and M. Kelly (ed) Women, men and the international division of labour (New York 1983).

Paglaban, E. 'Philippines Workers in the Export Industry' Pacific Research IX 3 and 4, 1978.

Safa, H. 'Runaway Shops and female employment: The search for cheap labor', SIGNS 7, 1981.

Santa Clara County, Annual Planning Report 1983-1984, Santa Clara County Office (Santa Clara 1984).

Semiconductor International, February 1982.

Siegal, L. 'Delicate Bonds: The Global semiconductor industry' Pacific Research 11, No.1, 1981.

Siegal, L. 'Orchestrating Dependency' Southeast Asia Chronicle 66, 1979.

Siegal, L. and R. Grossman 'Fairchild Assembles an Asian Empire' Pacific Research 9, No.2 1978.

Silcock, E. and E. Fisk (ed) The Political Economy of Independent Malaya (Berkeley 1963).

Strange, H. Rural Malay Women in Tradition and Transition (New York 1981).

Taplin, R. 'The Effects of the Electronics Industry on Rural Kinship Relations in Malaysia' Michigan Academician XVII, 1 Fall 1984(a).

Taplin, R. 'Women in World Market Factories: Asian women as preferred workers'. Paper presented to the American Association for the Advancement of Science, Sixty-fifth Annual Meeting, San Francisco, June 10-15, 1984(b).

Taplin, R. Women and World Development: A critique of the sociology of development, unpublished PhD dissertation (The London School of Economics 1984).

Wallerstein, I. The Capitalist World Economy (Cambridge 1979).

Warren, B. Imperialism: Pioneer of Capitalism (London 1980).

Women in Struggle, 'Malaya' Women in Struggle Collective (London 1978).

Wong, A. 'Planned Development, Social Stratification and the Sexual Division of Labor in Singapore', SIGNS Volume 7, No.2, 1981.

Wong, A. Economic Development and Women's Place, Women in Singapore Change International Report (London 1980).

References - Chapter Three

Alon, M. 'The Child and his Family in the Kibbutz: Second generation', in A. Jarus et al (ed) Children and Families in Israel (London 1970).

Bettleheim, B. Children of the Dream (London 1969).

Gerson, M. Family, Women and Socialization in the Kibbutz (Massachusetts 1978).

Gerson, M. 'The family in the Kibbutz' Journal of Child Psychology and Psychiatry, 15. 1974.

Hecht, D. and N. Yuval-Davis 'Ideology without revolution; women in Israel' Khamsin, 5, 1979.

Hurwitz, E. 'The Family in the Kibbutz' in P. Neubauer (ed), Children in Collectives, (Springfield 1965).

Irvine, E. The Family in the Kibbutz, Study Commission on the Family (London 1980).

Katzenelson-Rubashow, R. (ed) The Plough Women: Records of the Pioneer Women of Palestine (New York 1932).

Keller, S. 'The family in the Kibbutz: what lessons to us?' in M. Curtis and M. Chertoff (ed) Israel, Social Structure and Change (New Jersey 1973).

Laqueur, W. A History of Zionism (London 1972).

Leon, A. The Jewish Question: A Marxist Interpretation (New York 1970).

Leviatan, Uri, 'Work Life for the Older Person on the Kibbutz' Paper presented at the Tenth International Congress of Gerontology.

Maimon, A. 'Fifty Years of the Working Women's Movement' The Working Women in Israel, Women Worker's Council of Israel: Israel Information Centre, London, undated.

Mednick, S.M. 'Social Changes and Sex-Role Inertia: The Case of the Kibbutz' in S.M. Mednick et al (ed) Women and Achievement (London 1975).

Rayman, P. The Kibbutz Community and Nation Building (New Jersey 1981).

Rein, N. Daughters of Rachel, Women in Israel (London 1980).

Rosner, M. 'Emancipatory Use of New Technologies as Seen in the Kibbutzim' Jerusalem Quarterly 1987.

Rosner, M. 'Kibbutz Industrial Plants and the Challenge of Alienation' Paper presented to the XI World Congress of Sociology, International Sociological Assocation, New Dehli India 1986.

Rosner, M. 'Women in the Kibbutz: Changing Status and Concepts' Asian and African Studies, 3. 1967.

Rosner, M. and M. Palgi 'Family, familism and equality between the sexes' The Institute for Study and Research of the Kibbutz and the Cooperative Idea, University of Haifa, The Kibbutz Center, Haifa 1980.

Shain, R. The Functional Nature of the Sexual Division of Labour on an Israeli Kibbutz, Ph.D Dissertation, University of California, Berkeley, 1974.

Shur, S. and Y. Peres 'Equality and functional imperatives; another examination of distributive justice in the Israeli Kibbutz' The British Journal of Sociology, Volume XXXVII, No.3, September 1980.

Spiro, M. Gender and Culture: Kibbutz Women Revisited (Oklahoma 1980).

Tiger, L. and J. Shepher Women in the Kibbutz (New York 1975).

References - Chapter Four

Andors, P. The Unfinished Liberation of Chinese Women 1949-1980 (Bloomington 1983).

Andors, P. 'The 'Four Modernizations' and Chinese Policy on Women' Bulletin of Concerned Asian Scholars Volume 13 No.2 1981.

Andors, P. 'Politics of Chinese Development: The Case of Women 1960-1966' SIGNS Volume 2 No.1, 1976

Baker, H. Chinese Family and Kinship (New York 1979).

Beijing Review 'A Programme for Current Agricultural Work' Volume 25 No.24 1982(a).

Beijing Review 'Nanhai County: The Road Towards Prosperity' Volume 25 No.15 1982(b).

Business International Asian Research Report, Business Strategies for the People's Republic of China, Business International Corporation (Hong Kong 1980).

Byung-joon, A. 'The Political Economy of the People's Commune in China: Changes and Continuities' Journal of Asian Studies 34, 1975.

Chen, T. 'Working Women in China' Monthly Labor Review, Volume 15,1922.

China Trade and Economic Newsletter, No.309, Forty-eight Group of British Traders with China, 1981.

Croll, E. 'Women in Rural Development: The People's Republic of China' in Women in rural development: critical issues (Geneva 1980).

Croll, E. Feminism and Socialism in China (London 1978).

Davin, D. Women-Work and the Revolutionary Party in China (Oxford 1976).

Diamond, N. 'Collectivization, Kinship and the Status of Women in Rural China' Bulletin of Concerned Asian Scholars Volume 7, No.1 1975.

Fairbank, J. The United States and China (Cambridge, Mass. 1959).

Fei, H.T. Peasant Life in China - A Field Study of Country Life in the Yangtze Valley (London reprint 1980, 1939).

Gittings, J. 'Peking May Abolish Rural People's Communes' The Guardian September 4th 1981.

Johnson, K. Women the Family and Peasant Revolution in China (Chicago 1983).

Lippit, V. 'The People's Commune and China's New Development Strategy' Bulletin of Concerned Asian Scholars, Volume 13, No.3. 1981.

Moulder, F. Japan, China and the Modern World Economy - Towards a Re-interpretation of East Asian Development ca.1600-ca.1918 (Cambridge 1977).

Murray, N. 'Socialism and Feminism: Women and the Cuban Revolution: Part Two' Feminist Review 3, 1979.

Myrdal, G. Report from a Chinese Village (New York 1966).

Nee, V. 'Post-Mao Changes in South China Production Brigade' Bulletin of Concerned Asian Scholars, Volume 13, No.3 1981.

Parish, W. 'Socialism and the Chinese Peasant Family' Journal of Asian Studies Volume 34 No.3 1975.

Parish, W. and M. Whyte Village and Family Life in Contemporary China (Chicago 1978).

Purcell, V. The Boxer Uprising (Cambridge 1963).

Salaff, J. and J. Merkle 'Women and Revolution: The Lessons of the Soviet Union and China' in M. Young (ed) Women in China: Studies in Social Change and Feminism (Michigan 1973).

Sankar, A.P. 'The Evolution of Sisterhood in Traditional Chinese Society' Unpublished PhD Thesis, University of Michigan 1978.

So, A.Y. and M.T. Cheng 'Rural Industrialisation and Women's Liberation: A Study of Female Workers in the South China Silk District' Paper presented to the American Sociological Association, Toronto, August, 1981.

Stacy, J. Patriarchy and Socialist Revolution China (Berkeley 1983).

Stacy, J. 'When Patriarchy Kowtows: The Significance of the Chinese Family Revolution for Feminist Theory' in Z. Eisenstein (ed) Capitalist Patriarchy and the Case for Socialist Feminism (New York 1979).

Thorborg, M. 'Chinese Employment Policy in 1949-78 with Special Emphasis on Women in Rural Production' Chinese Economy Post-Mao, Congress of the United States (Washington D.C. 1978).

Topley, M. 'Marriage Resistance in Rural Kwangtung' in M. Wolf and R. Witke (ed) Women in Chinese Society (Stanford 1978).

Wang, B.L. Chan 'Chinese Women: The Relative Influences of Ideological Revolution, Economic Growth and Cultural Change?' in B. Lindsay (ed) Comparative Perspectives of Third World Women: The Impact of Race, Sex and Class (New York 1980).

Weinbaum, B. Pictures of Patriarchy (Boston 1982).

Weinbaum, B. Curious Courtship of Socialism and Women's Liberation (Boston 1978).

Weinbaum, B. 'Women in Transition to Socialism: Perspectives on the Chinese Case' The Review of Radical Political Economics Volume 8 No.1 1976.

Wolf, M. Revolution Postponed: Women in Contemporary China (Stanford 1985).

Wolf, M. and R. Witke Women in Chinese Society (Stanford 1975).

References - Conclusion

Hinton, W. Fanshen (New York 1966).

